RECIPES FROM
THE OTHER SIDE
OF THE STOVE

CONVERSATION STARTERS

CHEF ALEXIS HERNÁNDEZ

Copyright © 2024 Chef Alexis Hernández.

All rights reserved. No part of this book may be used or reproduced by any means, graphic, electronic, or mechanical, including photocopying, recording, taping or by any information storage retrieval system without the written permission of the author except in the case of brief quotations embodied in critical articles and reviews.

This book is a work of non-fiction. Unless otherwise noted, the author and the publisher make no explicit guarantees as to the accuracy of the information contained in this book and in some cases, names of people and places have been altered to protect their privacy.

Archway Publishing books may be ordered through booksellers or by contacting:

Archway Publishing
1663 Liberty Drive
Bloomington, IN 47403
www.archwaypublishing.com
844-669-3957

Because of the dynamic nature of the Internet, any web addresses or links contained in this book may have changed since publication and may no longer be valid. The views expressed in this work are solely those of the author and do not necessarily reflect the views of the publisher, and the publisher hereby disclaims any responsibility for them.

ISBN: 978-1-6657-5635-8 (sc)
ISBN: 978-1-6657-5636-5 (hc)
ISBN: 978-1-6657-5637-2 (e)

Library of Congress Control Number: 2024902319

Print information available on the last page.

Archway Publishing rev. date: 10/07/2024

This Book is Dedicated to Marty

For Marty, whose relentless advocacy has been the bedrock of my culinary life. Almost twenty-seven years ago, our paths intertwined, and since then, Marty has been a firm principal element of strength. He maintained confidence in me when I struggled to believe in myself. His unwavering trust in my cooking abilities led me to take a leap of faith and pursue formal culinary education by enrolling in culinary school with fear, eagerness, and determination. Even during the challenging times of studying and grappling with my ADHD, Marty's persistent cheering served as a constant reminder of the immense potential within me. Attending culinary school became a transformative journey, instilling in me a profound sense of purpose and confidence.

Marty has been my rock, providing invaluable encouragement, accompanying me to auditions, such as The Next Food Network Star, and supporting my endeavors on television shows like CNN's Sabores, Cutthroat Kitchen, and the Evilicious Tournament. Even in my failures, he pushed me forward, urging me to learn from my setbacks and use them to enhance myself and my craft.

For years, Marty persistently spurred me to gather and document not only the recipes used at my restaurant but also the culinary gems inspired by our travels and the creations I crafted at home. Inspired by his gentle nudges, I undertook the task of penning this cookbook.

The book of recipes I now present is not only a testament to Marty's persevering belief in my talent but also a reflection of the profound transformation I have experienced along this journey. Through Marty's unshakeable loyalty, I have rediscovered my own belief in my culinary abilities and cultivated immense growth and self-confidence, which now reside within me.

Marty, I want to express my deepest love and gratitude to you. You have been my guiding light and a beacon of single-minded support. I am forever filled with gratitude for your tenacious presence in my life.

With all my love,

Alexis

Foreword

When Alexis approached me to write the preface for his cookbook, I felt deeply honored and compelled to capture everything that resonates with me about this man. My goal is to provide you with a glimpse into the various aspects of Alexis that I've come to admire: his fervor and mastery in the culinary arts, his understanding of the intricate science behind gastronomy, and the diverse influences that have shaped his journey in creating a tapestry of rich cuisines. Before delving into these elements, let me share a personal anecdote that laid the foundation of our friendship and solidified my belief in the orchestration of fate.

Though a swift dozen years might make it seem distant, it was only in the recent past that we crossed paths in Los Angeles for Season 6 of the Next Food Network Star competition. Those days were a whirlwind of cooking, filming, and interviews, affording us little time for proper introductions. Amid the competition, I remained unaware of the skill sets of my fellow contestants, including Alexis's and his culinary prowess. During an initial challenge, I found myself struggling to keep up, and it was then that he graciously offered his assistance. I innocently inquired if he was familiar with the process of making a chive oil, later realizing that my question might have been unnecessary. His expertise shone through.

Skipping ahead through our shared swift eliminations, a silver lining emerged: a profound friendship blossomed over the course of weeks, perhaps even months (time often plays tricks on memory). Our swift exit from the show allowed us the opportunity to bond, explore LA, and immerse ourselves in its vibrancy. Our shared immigrant roots, with our families transplanted to America, wove threads of cultural heritage into our individual journeys. My status as a hometown local facilitated our escapades, and our conversations unveiled stories and experiences from our pasts. I marveled at Alexis's encyclopedic knowledge of the scientific intricacies of food during this time. Candid photos from our culinary explorations at restaurant Mozza and our creative endeavors in crafting meals from unconventional items like ramen noodles remain vivid in my memories. The period spent with him uncovered a cherished chapter and revealed an extraordinary soul and a masterful chef.

Alexis and I have candidly discussed our joint struggles with ADD and ADHD. While I often struggled to bring projects to fruition, Alexis's journey stands in stark contrast, marked by remarkable achievements. He has established a standout restaurant, amassed awards and accolades for Best Chef and Best Restaurant, conquered cooking competitions (including a victory on Alton Brown's Cutthroat Kitchen), and is now unveiling this cookbook—yet another milestone and layer of distinction in his illustrious career.

The pages of this book unfurl the perspectives of someone who has traversed the world and endeavors to share each facet with us. Alexis's collection of recipes spans the spectrum from delightful tidbits to intricate creations drawn from his restaurant, all tailored for the home cook and inspired by his travels.

I'm brimming with gratitude for the years of love, camaraderie, and encouragement that Alexis has brought into my life. His journey as Chef Alexis is nothing short of triumphant. Here's to you, my dearest Lexi! Let's raise a toast to your accomplishments, and may your story inspire those grappling with ADHD or ADD, and be a testament to unwavering determination and the limitless achievements possible through ambitious aspirations and a positive outlook.

Warm regards,
Chef Doreen Fang
CEO | Savor Acts

Alexis Hernández

PHOTOGRAPHY BY **CHRIS GIBBS**

Contents

Sips and Bites 1
    Burnt Caramel Old-Fashioned 2
    Orange and Rosemary Marinated Olives 4
    Millionaire's Bacon 5
    Easy Salsa 6
    Manhattan with a Twist 7
    Tinto de Verano 8
    Piedmont Driving Club Buttered Crackers 9
    Spicy Coconut Lime Chicken Satay 10

Kitchen Essentials 13
    Oven Blistered Cherry Tomatoes 14
    Quick Pickled Onions with Thyme and Garlic 16
    Perfect Hard-Boiled Eggs 18
    Easy Chicken Stock 19
    Flat Oven-Baked Bacon 20

Sauces and Salad Dressings 21
    Roasted Shallot Vinaigrette 22
    Dill Sauce 23
    Basic Pesto 24
    Blue Cheese Dressing 25
    Béarnaise Sauce 26
    Garlic Mayonnaise, a.k.a. Garlic Aioli 27

Starters 29
    Tomatoes with Brown Butter and Parmesan 30
    Easy Guacamole 32
    Pimento Cheese 34
    Bacon-Wrapped Chorizo-Stuffed Dates 35
    Baked Spinach and Artichoke Dip 36
    Caramelized Onion Dip 38
    Boursin Cheese and Pear Quesadilla 40
    Easy Hummus 41
    Grilled Elotes with Chipotle Cream and Cornbread Crumbs 42
    Crostini 43
    Blistered Tomato and Blue Cheese Bruschetta 44
    Prosciutto, Mozzarella, and Sage Brown Butter Crostini 46

Lunch 47
Sandwiches
    BLTs with Roasted Tomato and Garlic Mayonnaise 48
    Egg Salad Sandwich 50
    Chicken Pesto Sandwiches 52

Soups
    Carrot, Orange, and Ginger Soup 54
    Onion Soup 56
    Roasted Vegetable Soup 57

Salads
    Cucumber and Radish Salad with Red Onion and Dill 58
    Wedge Salad with Blue Cheese, Bacon, and Tomatoes 60
    Shaved Fennel with Onion and Torn Bread Croutons 62
    Beet Tartare 64

Sides and Vegetables 67
    Roasted Carrots with Cumin, Ginger, and Goat Cheese 68
    Hasselback Potatoes with Rosemary and Parmesan 70
    French Green Beans with Shallot Vinaigrette 72
    Sautéed Red Cabbage with Bacon and Gorgonzola 74
    Roasted Cauliflower with Tomatoes and Parmesan 76
    Braised Brussels Sprouts with Bourbon Soaked Cranberries 78
    Creamed Corn 80
    Garlicky Mashed Potatoes 82
    Creamed Pearl Onions with Lemon and Peanuts 84
    Roasted Root Vegetables 86
    Cinnamon Roasted Beets with Pistachio Butter 88

Entrees 91
    Brown Butter Ravioli 92
    Beef Filet with Goat Cheese and Shallot Vinaigrette 94
    Marty's Balsamic Marinated Flank Steak 96
    Roasted Chicken with Rosemary and Vegetables 97
    Spaghetti and Ricotta Meatballs 99
    Chicken Thighs with Hot Honey and Lemon 102
    Braised Lamb Shanks 104
    Peanut Butter BBQ Ribs 106
    Fried Chicken 108
    Sautéed Peas with Bacon and Dill 110

Desserts 113
    Toasted Coconut Cake 114
    Classic Chocolate Chip Cookie 116
    Flan 118
    Mock Apple Pie 120
    Olema's Caramel Flan Cake 121
    Chocolate Brownies 123
    Citrus Vanilla Bundt Cake 125
    Roasted Pears with Blue Cheese and Honey 127
    Mini Upside-Down Pineapple Cakes 129

Preface

I have the immense joy and gratitude to share my love for cooking and the recipes that have brought delight to those who have gathered around my table. As a professionally trained chef, I understand the allure of restaurant food: the intricate preparations, unique flavor pairings, and the artistry that goes into each dish. However, the intention of this cookbook is not to replicate the elaborate fuss of restaurant cuisine in the home kitchen. The recipes in this cookbook have been adapted from my restaurant, inspired by my travels, and crafted by me for intimate gatherings with friends at home. These recipes are specifically tailored for home cooks who already possess some kitchen skills and have a desire to expand their culinary knowledge. Furthermore, these recipes are crafted to foster personal expression and boost the confidence of the cooks in their own abilities.

The recipes span various categories, including appetizers, mains, and desserts, and reflect a diverse range of flavors and culinary traditions. While I firmly believe in the value of homemade meals, and while many recipes emphasize the joy of creating dishes from scratch, there are also instances where the use of store bought ingredients is incorporated, striking a balance between practicality and flavor.

May these recipes bring joy, foster connections, and spark meaningful conversations around your table.

Chef Alexis

Acknowledgments

First and most importantly, I want to thank God for bringing me from death to life through his son Jesus.

My mother Graciela and father Adalberto, I am deeply indebted to you both for instilling in me the belief that when we love and serve God, everything else He has in store for us will come in due time.

I would also like to express my sincere appreciation to my publisher, Archway, for their professionalism and invaluable assistance throughout the entire process of creating this cookbook.

To my sister Annette Hernandez and friend Stephen Smith, I am immensely grateful for your dedication in testing the recipes. Your commitment and feedback make you true champions in my book.

I extend my gratitude to Laura Kirk for her invaluable help in refining the written content in the book jacket. Thank you.

My heartfelt thanks go to Maria Sager, one of my dearest childhood friends, who not only helped me lay the tiles when I first opened the restaurant but also cheered me on as I tirelessly photographed the food for this book. Your unswerving loyalty and friendship mean the world to me.

I would like to extend my profound indebtedness to the following remarkable chefs, whose guidance and expertise have left an indelible impact on my culinary journey.

Chef Damon Kessler, I would like to extend a genuine appreciation to for your unwavering belief in me, both in the kitchen and as a friend. Your unwavering dedication and friendship have meant the world to me throughout our shared culinary experience. Your presence, your kindness, and your persistent belief in my potential as we worked together have uplifted me during challenging times.

Chef David Moeller, your commitment to advancing technical culinary skills has not gone unnoticed. Your relentless pursuit of excellence has challenged and motivated me to push my own boundaries in the kitchen. Thank you for imparting your expertise and instilling in me a passion for precision and innovation.

Chef Doreen Fang, from the moment we crossed paths on Food Network Star, your solid support and friendship have been invaluable to me. I am immensely thankful for the bond we have formed, for the friendship we share, and for the support you have freely given to me.

Chef Art Smith, your encouragement to audition for Top Chef, even though it didn't work out as planned, opened an unexpected door for me. The producers of Cutthroat Kitchen reaching out to me was a pivotal moment in my career, and I owe it to you for setting that course in motion. I am grateful for you.

To each of these incredible chefs, I express my deepest appreciation for the knowledge, guidance, and encouragement you have bestowed upon me. Your influence has shaped my culinary journey in immeasurable ways, and I am honored to have had the opportunity to learn from your expertise.

Chef Alexis Hernandez

Sips and Bites

For me, there's something special about starting a party surrounded by good company, delicious drinks, and mouthwatering small bites. It creates the perfect opportunity to engage in casual conversations and build excitement over a glass of wine or a well-crafted cocktail.

To make things even better, I've discovered the beauty of preparing small bites ahead of time. Whether it's on the same day or a few days prior, these delectable treats can be conveniently stored in the fridge until it's time to serve. It takes the pressure off and allows me to fully enjoy the moment without worrying about last-minute preparations.

Among my go-to favorites in this section are the Savory Orange and Rosemary Marinated Olives, with their delightful blend of citrusy tang and fragrant herbs, and the Piedmont Driving Club Crispy Buttered Crackers, which pair perfectly with any cocktail and disappear in seconds.

In fact, one of the secrets to effortless entertaining is having a handful of tried-and-true appetizers that never fail to impress. You don't have to reinvent the wheel each time you host a gathering. Instead, focus on perfecting a selection of four to five delicious appetizers that are easy to prepare and consistently deliver on taste. By showcasing these crowd-pleasers when friends come over, you can create a signature spread that becomes synonymous with your hospitality.

The following recipes have become staples in my entertaining repertoire. As you delve into the Sips and Bites section of this book, let yourself be inspired to create your own personal culinary delights from your own recipes.

Embrace the joy of hosting and the pleasure of sharing good food and drinks with cherished friends and family. These moments are what make life truly special. Cheers to unforgettable gatherings and the memories and conversations we create together!

Burnt Caramel Old-Fashioned

Seven years ago, I found myself at a hotel bar in London, exhausted after a long day of sightseeing. Hoping to unwind with a classic cocktail, I settled into a bar seat and ordered an old-fashioned. To my surprise, the drink that arrived had a unique and stylistic twist—a smoky, burnt sugar flavor that left me wanting another. For years, I tried to recreate that perfect burnt caramel old-fashioned, experimenting with different ingredients and flavor combinations. I couldn't quite figure out how to achieve that smoky burnt flavor until one day it hit me: my mom's burnt caramel syrup that she used in her famous flan. The syrup added a rich, smoky sweetness that was just right for the cocktail.

Makes 1 cocktail

Burnt Caramel Syrup
1/4 cup sugar
2 ounces water
1 tablespoon honey

Burnt Caramel Old Fashioned
2 1/2 ounces bourbon or rye

3/4 ounce burnt caramel syrup
3/4 ounce fresh orange juice
1/4 ounce lemon juice
3 drops bitters
splash of Antica vermouth
orange rind as a garnish

Burnt Caramel Syrup
In a small saucepan over medium heat, melt the sugar, stirring constantly until it turns a dark caramel color. Be cautious to avoid burning. Carefully add water (watch out for splatters), and continue stirring for a couple of minutes until well combined. Add honey and stir until fully dissolved. Set the burnt caramel syrup aside.

Burnt Caramel Old Fashioned
In a cocktail shaker, combine bourbon or rye, burnt caramel syrup, freshly squeezed orange juice, lemon juice, bitters, and a handful of ice. Shake vigorously for about 15 seconds to chill the mixture. Fill a rocks glass with fresh ice. Strain the cocktail into the glass. Add a splash of Antica vermouth to enhance the flavor profile.

Garnish the cocktail with a twist of orange rind by expressing the oils over the drink and dropping it into the glass.

Note: Antica vermouth is a sweet vermouth with dark notes of figs, cocoa, and a bouquet of almonds, and the finish has a bitter orange note that complements this cocktail perfectly.

Orange and Rosemary Marinated Olives

While I was in Buenos Aires years ago, I discovered a cigar bar that served bowls of marinated olives as a bar snack while you sipped on their specialty cocktails. I felt a bit self-conscious as an American asking for seconds and thirds of the tiny bowl of olives, but they were just that good. The olives were marinated with slices of orange and speckles of lemon zest, and this recipe brings me right back to that experience in Buenos Aries. These marinated olives are a fantastic accompaniment to cocktails—they're not quite an appetizer, but they're just enough to satisfy your cravings.

Makes 2 cups

1/2 cup olive oil
1/4 cup red wine vinegar
2 garlic cloves, minced
1 tablespoon fresh rosemary, minced
1 teaspoon dried oregano
1/2 teaspoon red pepper flakes
1/4 teaspoon freshly ground black pepper

1 lemon, zested
1 1/2 tablespoons honey
1 orange, peeled into strips with a vegetable peeler
1/4 cup chopped fresh parsley
2 cups mixed olives (Kalamata, Castelvetrano, Spanish olives)

In a large bowl, whisk the olive oil, red wine vinegar, minced garlic, minced rosemary, dried oregano, red pepper flakes, black pepper, lemon zest, and honey. Toss in the orange strips. Rinse the olives with warm water a couple of times and drain them. Add them to the marinade.

Cover the bowl with plastic, and let the olives sit in the refrigerator overnight. This will allow the flavors to meld together nicely. The olives can be kept in the refrigerator for up to two weeks. When you are ready to serve, remove the orange zest from the olives and discard.

Sprinkle chopped parsley over the olives before serving them.

Millionaire's Bacon

There's something about the combination of sweet and salty that just hits the spot. When it comes to sweet-and-salty snacks, there's nothing quite like this candied bacon. It's the perfect addition to deviled eggs, adding a chewy texture that takes this classic appetizer to the next level. When paired with burgers or sprinkled on salads, candied bacon adds a delicious crunch and a burst of flavor that is simply irresistible. Perhaps my favorite way to enjoy candied bacon is as a standalone snack, served with cocktails.

Makes 10 pieces of bacon

Sugar Dredge
1/2 cup brown sugar
1/2 cup white sugar
2 tablespoons cinnamon
1 tablespoon ground ginger

1 teaspoon chili powder (optional)

Bacon
10 strips thick-cut bacon

Preheat oven to 375 degrees F.

Sugar Dredge
Mix together the dredge ingredients and whisk until all the dry ingredients are combined.

Candied Bacon
Roll each strip of bacon in the sugar mixture, ensuring that it is fully coated, then shake off the excess sugar. Next, place the bacon on a sheet pan lined with parchment paper and bake at 375 degrees F for 15 to 20 minutes, or until it is caramelized. (Please note that the baking time may vary depending on your oven.) Once the bacon is done, immediately remove it from the pan and place it on a sheet of parchment paper, making sure that the strips don't touch while they cool or they will stick together. After the bacon has cooled, you can enjoy it.

If you're making the candied bacon ahead of time, allow it to cool completely, then spray it with nonstick cooking spray and wrap it in parchment paper. Store the wrapped bacon in an airtight container in the refrigerator for up to three days. Before serving, let the bacon come to room temperature for about an hour.

Note: Below are a few suggestions on how to serve this delicious candied bacon.

- As a burger topping: Add a strip or two of the candied bacon on top of a juicy burger for an extra burst of flavor and crunch.

- In salads: Crumble the candied bacon over a salad for a sweet and savory crunch.

- With brunch: Serve the candied bacon alongside your favorite breakfast items, such as pancakes or waffles, for a decadent treat.

Easy Salsa

Fresh salsa is often overlooked because it's seen as a hassle to make, but this recipe is here to change that. By simplifying the process and leaving the tomato skins intact, we've made it convenient to whip up delicious homemade salsa. Leaving the skins on not only saves you time and effort but also adds a subtle thickness to the salsa, enhancing its texture without compromising the vibrant flavors of ripe tomatoes.

Serves 4-6

6 ripe tomatoes
1 small white onion, finely chopped
1 jalapeño pepper, seeded and finely chopped
1/4 cup fresh cilantro leaves, chopped

3 garlic cloves, minced
juice of 1 lime
1/2 teaspoon ground cumin
1/2 teaspoon kosher salt
1/4 teaspoon freshly ground black pepper

First, cut out and discard the tough core at the stem end, then chop the tomatoes into small pieces. In a mixing bowl, combine the chopped tomatoes, onion, jalapeño pepper, cilantro, minced garlic, lime juice, cumin, salt, and black pepper. Mix well. Transfer half of the mixture to a food processor or blender and pulse a few times until it reaches a chunky purée consistency. Add the puréed mixture back into the bowl with the remaining chunky tomato mixture. Stir until all the ingredients are thoroughly combined. Taste the salsa and adjust the seasonings according to your preference. Allow the salsa to sit for at least 30 minutes before serving to allow the flavors to meld together. You can also refrigerate it for a few hours to enhance the taste further.

Serve the salsa with tortilla chips.

Note:

- By combining both puréed and chopped tomatoes in the salsa, you achieve a balance of textures. The puréed tomatoes provide a smooth and consistent base, while the chopped tomatoes add a chunkier texture. This combination enhances the overall mouthfeel and enjoyment of the salsa.

Manhattan with a Twist

When we lived on our farm, I had the pleasure of spending many a weekend with my chef friends. One weekend, we decided to make cocktails and experiment with different ingredients to create new flavors. Some of the concoctions we tried were unappetizing, while others were simply amazing. This cocktail, however, stood out from the rest and reminded me of a B52. After much deliberation, we settled on using 1/2 ounce of Kahlúa coffee liqueur and 1/2 ounce of Baileys Irish Cream. The velvety texture and subtle complexity of the liqueurs complemented the warmth and depth of the whiskey. Overall, this cocktail is a perfect example of how experimentation can lead to delicious and unexpected flavor combinations.

Makes 1 cocktail

2 ounces bourbon or rye bourbon
1 ounce Antica vermouth
1/2 ounce coffee liqueur like Kahlúa

1/2 ounce Baileys Irish Cream
2 dashes Angostura bitters
1 Luxardo maraschino cherry

To a cocktail shaker filled with ice, add the bourbon, vermouth, Kahlúa coffee liqueur, Baileys Irish Cream and bitters. Stir with a bar spoon until it is thoroughly chilled. Strain into a martini glass and garnish with the Luxardo cherry.

Tinto de Verano

Tinto de Verano, known as the beloved "red wine of summer," holds a cherished place in Spanish beverage culture for its refreshing simplicity, especially during the scorching summer months. It was introduced to me by a dear Spanish friend who inquired about the fate of a lingering half bottle of red wine on my kitchen counter. Initially, I had planned to reserve it solely for cooking, but my friend's inspiration struck, urging me to enjoy it as a cocktail instead. This was my introduction to the captivating allure of Tinto de Verano. By blending leftover red wine with carbonated lemon-lime soda, the result is a fizzy and revitalizing libation, perfect for quenching thirst on warm days. It really reminds me of a paired down red sangria. Served over ice and garnished with a slice of lemon or orange, it's a delightful choice that promises not to disappoint.

Makes 1 cocktail

1 part red wine (such as Rioja or any medium-bodied red wine)
1 part carbonated lemon-lime soda

lemon or orange slices for garnish (optional)

Fill a glass with ice cubes, leaving some space at the top for the garnishes, if using. Pour equal parts of red wine and carbonated lemon soda into the glass. You can adjust the ratio based on your taste preferences. Gently stir the mixture with a spoon to combine the wine and soda. Garnish with a slice of lemon or orange, if desired.

Note:

- Opt for a medium-bodied red wine, such as Rioja, Tempranillo, or any other red wine that you enjoy. The choice of wine will impact the flavor profile of the drink, so feel free to experiment with different varieties to find your preferred taste.

Piedmont Driving Club Buttered Crackers

These delectable cocktail accompaniments have a fascinating origin story. As the tale goes, one day at the Capital City Club, the chef found himself without oyster crackers to serve with soup. In a moment of culinary inspiration, the chef took some saltine crackers and tossed them with clarified butter, and the result was an instant hit. I like to dress them up and add some cumin or fennel seeds to them for a different variation, or spice them up with some dried red pepper flakes.

Serves 6-8

2 sticks butter
48 saltine crackers

Kosher salt

Preheat oven to 400 degrees F.

Cut the sticks of butter into 1/2-inch squares and melt the butter in a pan over medium fire. Once foam starts to form, remove it with a spoon to clarify the butter. This process should take about 5 to 7 minutes. This leaves you with clarified butter. Place the saltines in a bowl and pour the clarified butter over them. Gently toss the saltines to coat them with butter, allowing some of the clarified butter to soak into the crackers. Carefully spread the saltines in a single layer on a sheet pan lined with parchment paper. Sprinkle kosher salt on top. Bake them for 3 to 4 minutes.

Note:

- For a spicy twist, you can add a pinch of red pepper flakes or cayenne pepper to the buttered saltines before baking.

- After the saltines have cooled, store them in an airtight container to maintain their crispiness.

Spicy Coconut Lime Chicken Satay

As a chef, I love discovering new flavor combinations and experimenting with different ingredients in the kitchen. I've tried countless variations over the years, but I finally landed on a recipe that is both easy to make and incredibly delicious. This recipe is inspired by the bold and vibrant flavors of Southeast Asia. While not strictly traditional, the juicy strips of marinated chicken are flavored with a rich mixture of coconut milk, soy sauce, cayenne, and lime juice, giving them a spicy and tangy kick.

Serves 4-6

1 1/2 pounds chicken breast, cut into 4-inch strips
1 cup unsweetened coconut milk
1/4 teaspoon kosher salt
1/2 teaspoon cayenne pepper
1 tablespoon grated ginger
4 tablespoons soy sauce
2 teaspoons brown sugar
3 tablespoons fresh lime juice
1/4 cup roasted peanuts, chopped
bamboo skewers, soaked in water for 30 minutes

Preheat your grill or grill pan to medium-high fire.

In a mixing bowl, combine the coconut milk, salt, cayenne pepper, grated ginger, soy sauce, brown sugar, and lime juice. Whisk together until well combined. Reserve 6 ounces of the marinade for serving.

Add the chicken strips to the marinade and toss until well coated. Cover the bowl with plastic wrap and marinate in the refrigerator for at least 30 minutes or up to 2 hours. Thread the marinated chicken strips onto the bamboo skewers. Grill the chicken skewers for 5 to 6 minutes on each side, or until the chicken is cooked through and slightly charred. Place the skewers on a serving platter and sprinkle the chopped peanuts over the top of the chicken.

Serve the chicken skewers with the reserved marinade and a side of soy sauce.

Note:

- The marinade plays a crucial role in enhancing the flavor and tenderness of the chicken. The combination of coconut milk, soy sauce, and acidic lime juice helps tenderize the chicken by breaking down proteins through a process called denaturation. The marinade also allows the flavors to penetrate the meat, resulting in a more flavorful and juicy end result.

- When grilling the chicken skewers, the high heat promotes the Maillard reaction. This chemical reaction between amino acids and reducing sugars in the marinade leads to the development of desirable browning, aromas, and flavors. It contributes to the charred exterior and adds depth to the overall taste profile of the dish.

Kitchen Essentials

In the culinary world, the significance of kitchen essentials cannot be overstated. Within a professional kitchen brigade, each member holds a specific responsibility in preparing the foundational components that underpin every dish. From simple tasks like crisping bacon for a classic BLT to more intricate techniques like perfecting a crostini, these elements form the bedrock of culinary excellence in your own kitchen.

In addition to these fundamental components, skilled chefs also create an array of sauces, stocks, and flavorful dressings that serve as the building blocks for countless dishes. These culinary basics act as the backbone of flavors, elevating taste profiles and enhancing the overall dining experience.

In the Kitchen Essentials section of this cookbook, I have curated a selection of these vital building blocks that I personally rely on to enhance the dishes I prepare at home. While they may not stand alone as complete recipes, their value lies in their ability to elevate the flavor and presentation of your other dishes. They provide a palette of vibrant colors, intriguing textures, and an extra layer of interest to your favorite recipes.

Oven Blistered Cherry Tomatoes

This tomato recipe is a fantastic flavor-building addition to any dish that needs a pop of color and acidity. Similar to many of the recipes listed in this section, these cherry tomatoes don't stand on their own but rather amplify the flavors of the other components around them. You can use them as a replacement for tomatoes on a burger, add them in an omelet, or on top of grilled fish, pork, or lamb to add a burst of acidity that will elevate the dish. I prefer to use these tomatoes due to their vibrant dark red color and their ability to refresh and cleanse the palate when consuming dishes that are rich in fat.

Makes 2 1/2 cups

2 pints cherry tomatoes, cut in half
1 teaspoon kosher salt
2 teaspoons granulated white sugar

3 tablespoons Worcestershire sauce
1 teaspoon dried thyme
Olive oil
Balsamic vinegar

Preheat oven to 375 degrees F.

On a half-sheet pan lined with parchment paper, combine all the ingredients except the balsamic vinegar and toss together. Arrange the cherry tomatoes in a single layer on the sheet pan, and if necessary, use two pans to avoid overcrowding.

Roast in a preheated 375 degree F oven for 25 minutes, then use a spatula to flip the tomatoes and spread them out evenly on the pan. Continue to roast for an additional 20 to 25 minutes until the tomatoes are caramelized. Remove the pan from the oven and deglaze the roasted tomatoes with 3 to 4 shakes of balsamic vinegar. Use a spatula to scrape the tomatoes and caramelized sugars from the parchment paper, making sure to combine the browned bits from the pan with the tomatoes.

The roasted tomatoes can be stored in an airtight container in the fridge for up to a week.

Note:

- During the roasting process, the sugar in the recipe will caramelize and create dark, almost burnt-looking spots on the parchment paper. This is called fond. To extract the deep, rich flavor of the fond, deglaze the pan with balsamic vinegar. This will coax the flavor compounds off the parchment paper and onto the roasted tomatoes.

- Mix into a pasta sauce for added depth of flavor.

- As a filling for omelets or quiches.

Quick Pickled Onions with Thyme and Garlic

These tangy, slightly sweet onions act as a flavor booster that cuts through the richness of a dish, leaving your palate refreshed and ready for the next bite. Pickled onions are a versatile condiment that can be used in a variety of dishes, including burgers, beef roasts, pork chops, tacos, grain bowls, and salads dressed with dairy-based dressings.

Makes about 2 cups

1 medium red onion	**1 teaspoon dried thyme**
1/2 cup water	**1 cup apple cider vinegar**
1/2 cup granulated sugar	**or white vinegar**
2 tablespoons freshly grated ginger	**4 garlic cloves, thinly sliced**
1 teaspoon kosher salt	**1 teaspoon black peppercorns**
	1 bay leaf

Take your onion, remove the root end, and slice thinly on a mandoline. Place the red onion in a large Mason jar or heatproof container. In a saucepan, combine the water, sugar, ginger, salt, thyme, vinegar, garlic, peppercorns, and bay leaf. Bring the mixture to a boil, stirring occasionally to ensure the sugar and salt dissolve. Pour the hot vinegar mixture over the sliced onions in the jar, ensuring the onions are completely submerged. Allow the mixture to cool to room temperature, then cover the jar and refrigerate for at least 1 hour before using. The pickled onions will keep in the refrigerator for up to two weeks.

Note:

- These pickled onions are a great addition to tacos, sandwiches, salads, and more.

- Use the pickled onions with grilled meats for added acidity.

- If you don't have whole black peppercorns, you can substitute ground black pepper.

- You can also add additional spices like cinnamon or cloves for extra flavor in the pickling solution.

Perfect Hard-Boiled Eggs

One of the questions I am frequently asked is how to cook eggs without ending up with greenish yolks. During my culinary school days, a British chef taught me a cooking technique that was a game-changer. Since then, I have used this foolproof method to cook eggs and have never been disappointed. This technique ensures that the egg whites come out perfectly firm while the yolks retain their moist and beautiful yellow texture. With this method, you can cook eggs with perfect results every time.

Makes 12 eggs

1 dozen eggs   **Water**

Place the eggs in a pot and cover them completely with water so that there is about 1 inch of water above the eggs.

Bring the eggs to a boil. As soon as the pot boils, take it off the fire, cover it with a lid, and set a timer for 10 minutes. Once the timer goes off, drain the hot water from the pot and shake the eggs in the pan to crack them a little. Fill the pan with cold tap water. Allow the eggs sit in the water for about 2 minutes before you begin peeling them.

Take peel an egg, crack it on its side and then roll it gently on the counter to loosen the shell. Start peeling the shell from the wider part of the egg (not the pointy side of the egg) using your finger. The wider part of the egg should have lots of room between the shell and the egg white, making it the perfect place to begin peeling. If you have difficulty removing the shell, dip the egg in cold water and continue removing the shell.

Easy Chicken Stock

As the winter air sets in, there's nothing quite like a warm bowl of soup to comfort and nourish the body. But what separates a good soup from a great one? The answer lies in the stock. Homemade chicken stock is the backbone of many soups, stews, and sauces, providing a rich and complex flavor that can't be matched by store bought varieties. This recipe for chicken stock is simple and cost-effective, using chicken wings and a handful of aromatic vegetables and herbs to create a base that's both flavorful and versatile. I freeze the stock in ice cube trays and store them in a plastic bag for easy use in making quick pan sauces.

Makes 4 quarts

3 pounds chicken wings
2 large onions, chopped
4 garlic cloves, smashed
6 celery stalks, chopped
6 large carrots, peeled and chopped

2 bay leaves
10 peppercorns
2 sprigs fresh thyme
16 cups water
2 teaspoons kosher salt

To a large pot, add the chicken wings, onion, garlic, celery, carrot, bay leaves, black peppercorns, and thyme. Pour in the water and add the salt. If the water doesn't cover the vegetables and chicken, add more until it is covered. Bring the pot to a boil, then reduce the heat to low and let the stock simmer for 3 to 4 hours covered with a lid.

Remove the pot from the stove and let it cool slightly. Strain the stock. Next, use a ladle or a large spoon to scoop out as much of the visible fat as possible from the top of the stock. You can also use a fat separator or a gravy strainer to remove the fat more efficiently. Once you have removed as much fat as possible, strain the stock through a fine-mesh strainer or cheesecloth into a clean container.

Let the stock cool completely, then refrigerate it for several hours or overnight. As the stock cools, the remaining fat will rise to the top and solidify, making it easy to remove. Simply skim off the hardened fat with a spoon or use a paper towel to blot it off.

Note:

- Store the stock in an airtight container in the refrigerator for up to 5 days.

- To freeze the stock, let it cool to room temperature and pour it into freezer-safe containers or plastic bags. To stack the frozen bags easily, it's best to lay them flat in the freezer while they freeze.

- Label the containers or bags with the date and freeze for up to 6 months.

- Thaw the frozen stock in the refrigerator overnight before using it.

- For an easy way to portion the stock, consider using ice cube trays. Once the stock has cooled, pour it into the trays, then freeze until solid. Pop out the cubes and store them in a labeled zip-top bag in the freezer for up to 3 months.

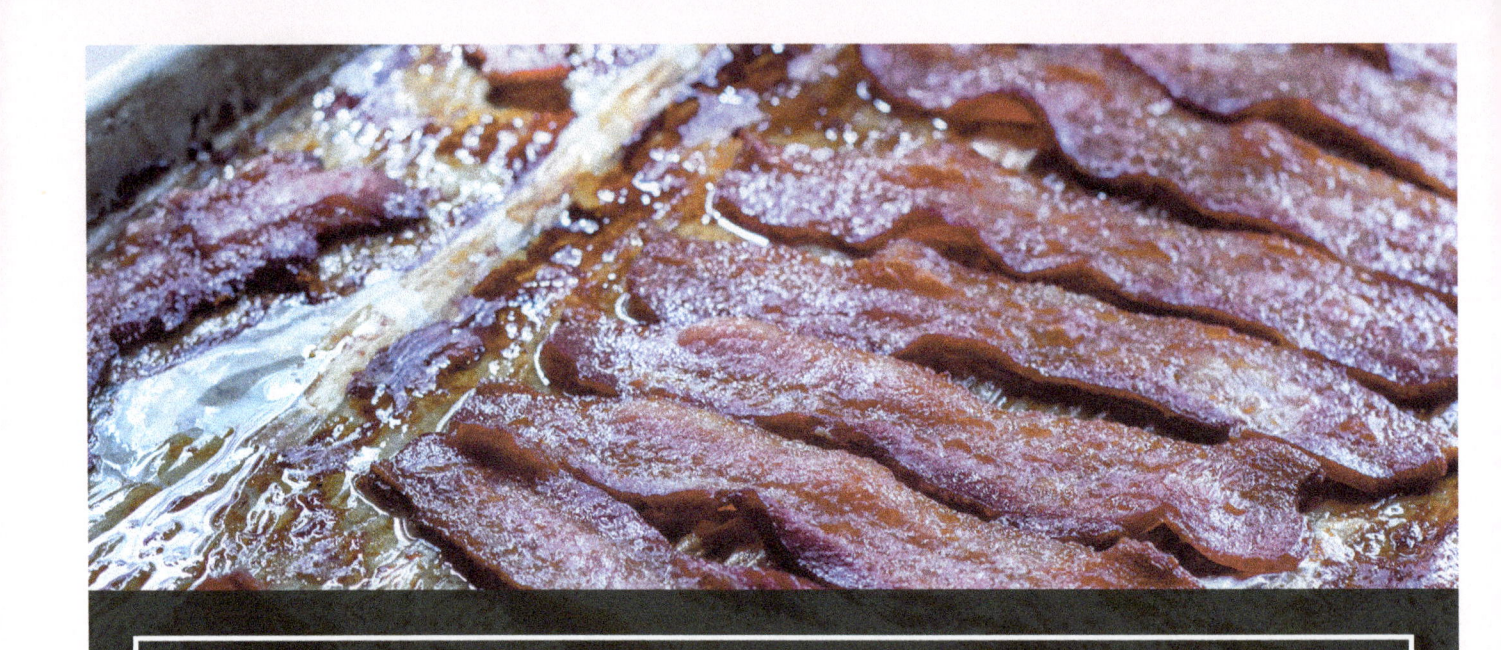

Flat Oven-Baked Bacon

Looking for a hassle-free way to cook bacon that won't make a mess of your kitchen stove? Try this technique: lay the bacon flat on a parchment-lined sheet pan and bake it in the oven. Not only will your bacon stay flat, but it will also be crispy and evenly cooked, without any splatters or grease stains to clean up on the stove top. Plus, you can make a big batch a day or two ahead of time and gently reheat it in the microwave for a quick breakfast, or use it to make the crispiest BLT sandwiches you've ever tasted.

Makes 16 slices of bacon

16 slices thick-cut bacon

Preheat oven to 400 degrees F.

Line a sheet pan with parchment paper and lay the bacon flat on it. Do not overlap the bacon.

Cook the bacon in the middle rack for 15 to 18 minutes until the bacon is crispy.

Drain the bacon grease and save it for cooking later. Remove the bacon to a plate lined with a paper towel.

Note: How to store the bacon and utilize the leftover bacon oil.

- To store the cooked bacon, wrap it in parchment paper and keep it in an airtight container or plastic bag in the refrigerator for up to 3 days. When you're ready to eat, you can reheat the bacon in the oven or microwave.

- Don't throw away the leftover bacon oil! You can strain it and store it in an airtight container in the refrigerator for up to a month. Use it to cook eggs, sauté vegetables, or add flavor to roasted potatoes or other dishes. Use it in dishes where you want that smoky, savory taste.

Sauces and Salad Dressings

Roasted Shallot Vinaigrette

This versatile vinaigrette is about to become your new secret weapon in the kitchen. Sure, roasting shallots takes a bit of extra time, but the end result is absolutely worth the effort. The flavors intensify, creating a caramelized sweetness that adds a depth and complexity. You can prepare this vinaigrette up to three days in advance, saving you valuable time without compromising on taste. Now, I know we often associate vinaigrettes with salads, but this one goes beyond the greens. It's incredibly versatile and pairs perfectly as a finishing touch for grilled meats like steaks, chicken, or lamb. Trust me—it adds that extra layer of flavor that will leave your taste buds begging for more.

Makes 1 cup

3 shallots, sliced 1/4 inch thick
1 garlic clove
1 star anise or 2 whole cloves (optional)
3/4 cup olive oil

3 tablespoons balsamic vinegar
2 teaspoons Dijon mustard
1/2 teaspoon kosher salt
1/2 teaspoon ground black pepper

Preheat oven to 325 degrees F.

Put the shallots, garlic, olive oil and star anise in a large ramekin. Place the ramekin on a sheet pan and roast it uncovered for 30 to 45 minutes or until the shallots are roasted and caramelized. Throw away the star anise or the cloves and allow the shallot oil mixture to cool completely. Then put the oil, shallots, and garlic clove into a small food processor and turn it on. Slowly add the balsamic vinegar, mustard, salt, and black pepper until the mixture is emulsified.

Note:

-This can be held in the refrigerator for up to 5 days. If the sauce separates while it is being held in the refrigerator, whisk it in a bowl until it comes back together.

Dill Sauce

This versatile condiment boasts a creamy texture, vibrant herbs, and a touch of tang, making it the ultimate companion to elevate the taste of your favorite dishes. I used to serve this at my restaurant for years in many renditions. We would serve it with our grilled fish, with seafood, and with soft-shell crabs when they were in season.

Makes 1 3/4 cups

1 cup mayonnaise
1/4 cup sour cream
2 tablespoons milk
2 teaspoons white vinegar
1 tablespoon fresh lemon juice
3 tablespoons fresh dill, chopped

1 tablespoon fresh parsley leaves, chopped
2 garlic cloves, minced
1 teaspoon Worcestershire sauce
1 teaspoon Dijon mustard
1/4 teaspoon kosher salt

In a bowl, mix all of the ingredients together. Let it sit for 30 minutes in the refrigerator or overnight before using. Taste the sauce and adjust the seasoning with Kosher salt according to your preference. Add salt gradually, tasting as you go, until the desired flavor is achieved.

Note:

-Dill sauce pairs well with grilled chicken, roasted potatoes, fish tacos, veggie dip, grilled salmon, sandwiches and wraps, deviled eggs, Greek gyros, grilled vegetables, and as a salad dressing.

Basic Pesto

Pesto, an Italian classic with a vibrant history and fresh flavors, is a versatile sauce that elevates the taste of meats, sandwiches, wraps, and pastas. Its herbaceous essence adds a delightful Mediterranean charm to grilled chicken, succulent shrimp, and juicy steak. Moreover, pesto shines in pasta salads and spreads, offering a delightful mayo alternative for sandwiches. Discover the endless possibilities as pesto brings a burst of freshness to your culinary creations.

Makes 1 cup

2 cups fresh basil leaves
1/2 cup grated Parmesan cheese
1/2 cup walnuts or pine nuts
3 cloves garlic

1/2 cup extra virgin olive oil
1/2 teaspoon kosher salt
1/2 teaspoon freshly ground black pepper

In a food processor or blender, combine the fresh basil leaves, grated Parmesan cheese, walnuts or pine nuts, garlic cloves, salt, and pepper. Pulse the ingredients a few times to break them down. Gradually pour in the extra virgin olive oil while the food processor is running. Continue blending until the mixture becomes a smooth and creamy paste. Taste the pesto and adjust the seasoning as desired, adding more salt and pepper if needed.

Note:

- When exposed to air, pesto can undergo oxidation, causing it to darken in color. To minimize this, press a layer of plastic wrap directly onto the surface of the pesto or drizzle a thin layer of olive oil on top before sealing the container. This barrier helps reduce contact with air and slows down the oxidation process.

- Freezing helps retain the flavors and colors of the ingredients. It is best to freeze pesto in ice cube trays, allowing for easy portioning and thawing when needed.

Blue Cheese Dressing

This blue cheese dressing is one of the best and easiest to make in my experience as a professional chef. I really enjoy how the cream cheese adds a sticky viscosity to the dressing and how the scallions add a certain flavor that makes this one of my go-to dressings for more than just lettuces. I like to use this with burgers or chicken wings or serve it up with some kettle chips.

Makes 3 cups

1 cup mayonnaise
8 ounces sour cream
8 ounces blue cheese at room temperature
8 ounces cream cheese at room temperature
6 scallions, white and green parts minced

2 tablespoons white vinegar
3 tablespoons Dijon mustard
2 tablespoons Worcestershire sauce
2 tablespoons garlic powder
1 teaspoon Kosher salt
5 dashes hot sauce

Add all ingredients to a bowl and blend with a fork until combined.

If you find the mixture too thick, add one tablespoon of water and mix until your desired consistency is achieved.

Note:

- This can be made 3 days ahead and kept in the refrigerator for up to 4 days.

Béarnaise Sauce

Traditionally enjoyed alongside juicy steaks, succulent roasted meats, and delicate fish, béarnaise sauce adds a touch of elegance to your favorite dishes. This classic recipe combines the reduction of vinegar, shallots, and tarragon with the velvety embrace of egg yolks and butter. Once you've honed this technique, you'll discover a multitude of uses and creative applications for this versatile sauce. Personally, I find myself irresistibly dipping crispy French fries into a small ramekin of this culinary gem.

Makes 1 1/2 cups

1/4 cup white wine
1/4 cup white wine vinegar
2 shallots, minced
3 teaspoons dried tarragon

3 egg yolks
2 sticks (1 cup) unsalted butter, at room temperature
1/4 teaspoon kosher salt

Melt the butter in a saucepan over medium heat; set aside. In a separate pan over medium heat, combine the white wine, white wine vinegar, minced shallots, and dried tarragon. Cook until the liquid has reduced, leaving about 3 tablespoons. Remove from heat and set aside. Fill a pot with water and bring it to a simmer. Place a stainless steel bowl on top of the pot, ensuring that the water doesn't touch the bottom of the bowl. This will create a double boiler setup. Place the egg yolks in the stainless steel bowl and whisk them vigorously until they have doubled in size. This should take about 5 to 7 minutes. Slowly pour the melted butter into the egg yolks while whisking continuously to create an emulsion. Add the shallot mixture to the emulsion and whisk until well combined. Stir in the kosher salt. If the sauce is too thick, add 1 tablespoon of water and whisk to loosen it.

Serve the béarnaise sauce immediately as a delightful accompaniment to steak, roasted meats, fish, or even as a dip for French fries.

Note:

- In some kitchen applications, the sauce is strained to remove any solids in the sauce, however, that is completely optional. I like the chunkiness the shallots lend to the sauce.

Garlic Mayonnaise, a.k.a. Garlic Aioli

Garlic, often underestimated, holds an incredible power to enhance dishes with its aromatic and savory qualities, a truth well-known to most home cooks. My culinary school days led me on a captivating journey into the world of garlic confit—a culinary technique that unveiled the true magic of the humble garlic clove. Slowly roasting garlic in oil at a low temperature brought forth its transformative flavors. It was during this exploration that I uncovered the culinary gem of garlic mayonnaise, also known as garlic aioli. This velvety spread, with its creamy and flavorful profile, takes sandwiches, burgers, and garlic bread to new heights of culinary delight. Let's not forget its irresistible charm as a dip for fries!

Makes 2 cups

Roasted Garlic:
1 1/2 cups peeled garlic
3 cups or more of olive oil or canola oil
2 sprigs rosemary

Garlic Mayonnaise:
15-20 roasted garlic cloves
2 cups prepared mayonnaise
2 tablespoons fresh lemon juice
1 teaspoon kosher salt

Preheat oven to 250 degrees F.

Place the peeled garlic cloves and rosemary sprigs into a spacious ovenproof casserole dish, ensuring there is ample room to accommodate the garlic comfortably. Pour enough olive oil into the dish to fully cover the garlic and rosemary.

Bake in a preheated oven at 250 degrees F for 2 hours, or until the garlic cloves yield to the tines of a fork. Use a slotted spoon to remove the garlic cloves from the oil, making sure to save the oil for cooking later in the week.

Place the garlic cloves in a bowl. Use a fork to mash the roasted garlic cloves until they form a paste-like consistency. Add the mayonnaise, lemon juice, and kosher salt to the bowl with the mashed garlic. Whisk the ingredients together until they are thoroughly combined. Transfer the garlic mayonnaise to a storage container and refrigerate.

It can be stored in the refrigerator for up to 7 days.

Note:

- Garlic confit operates on the principle of low-temperature cooking, typically around 200 to 250 degrees F (93 to 121 degrees C). This gentle heat encourages the enzymatic reactions within the garlic cloves, promoting the breakdown of complex carbohydrates into simpler sugars.

- The garlic develops a sweeter taste while its pungent compounds, such as allicin, are partially converted into milder, aromatic compounds.

- The slow cooking process allows the flavors of the garlic to infuse the oil, creating a rich and flavorful base for various culinary applications.

Starters

Starters are an integral part of any meal or gathering, playing a crucial role in setting the tone and making a lasting impression on your guests. A starter is intended to awaken the appetite and set the tone for the meal. It is typically a smaller portion of food, often featuring flavorful ingredients and creative presentations. Starters can include a wide range of dishes such as soups, salads, bruschetta, dips, or small plates with various ingredients like seafood, vegetables, or meats. They provide an excellent opportunity to showcase your culinary skills and creativity, encompassing a wide range of options from finger foods and small plates to dips and spreads.

Well-crafted appetizers have the power to whet your guests' appetites and leave them eagerly anticipating the rest of the meal.

In the Sips and Bites section, you'll discover a variety of finger foods specifically crafted for parties and social gatherings. These delicious bite-sized treats are designed to be conveniently enjoyed while standing and mingling with others. They range from simple snacks to canapés, each boasting bold flavors and classic ingredient combinations. The selection provided here represents a sample of starters that I have personally enjoyed and frequently share with guests when they visit my home.

Tomatoes with Brown Butter and Parmesan

Back when I lived on our farm, my love for growing tomatoes led me to cultivate a variety of them, but the beefsteak tomato held a special place in my heart. There's a certain magic in plucking a fresh tomato straight from the vine and transforming it into a salad using just a handful of ingredients. This recipe is not only a personal favorite of mine, but also a cherished memory. The combination of the rich and nutty brown butter, paired with the tangy balsamic vinegar, creates a harmonious blend that beautifully complements the juicy and sweet beefsteak tomatoes. To elevate the flavors even further, I like to add freshly chopped tarragon, which imparts an additional layer of freshness. It's a simple, yet elegant dish that suits any occasion, and every time I make it, it transports me back to those nostalgic days on our farm.

Serves 4

2-3 large beefsteak tomatoes
kosher salt
1 cup (2 sticks) butter
1 tablespoon fresh tarragon, chopped

2 tablespoons balsamic vinegar
1/4 cup freshly grated Parmesan cheese
2 tablespoons chives, minced

Tomatoes: Core the top of the tomatoes and slice them into 1/3-inch thick rounds. Place an equal amount of sliced tomatoes on four plates and sprinkle a little kosher salt over the top of all the tomatoes. Set aside.

Brown Butter: Cut the butter into small squares to help it melt quickly. In a small saucepan over medium fire, melt the butter. Stir the butter until you begin to see small caramelized bits that look like black pepper on the bottom of the pan, about 3 to 4 minutes. Remove the pan from the fire and pour the brown butter into a small heatproof bowl, being sure to scrape any black specks from the bottom of the pan. Then add the tarragon and balsamic vinegar to the bowl and whisk until the balsamic vinegar and brown butter have emulsified. Pour some of the brown butter sauce and cheese over each of the tomatoes.

Sprinkle the chives over the tomatoes and serve immediately.

Note:

- Keep an eye on the butter while it's cooking to prevent it from burning.

- Be sure to serve the dish immediately after adding the sauce and cheese, as the tomatoes will become watery and lose their texture if they sit for too long.

- Try adding a squeeze of fresh lemon juice to the brown butter sauce for a bright, acidic contrast to the rich butter instead of the tangy balsamic.

Easy Guacamole

In my mid-twenties, I had the pleasure of spending a week in Puerto Vallarta, where I discovered a beach known as the Blue Chairs. Nestled near that beach was a charming hotel, where I indulged in their unforgettable happy hour. There, under the warm glow of the setting sun, I was treated to guacamole prepared by two talented women. The flavors were a symphony of lime juice, creamy avocados, crunchy radishes, zesty onions, and a touch of salt. Needless to say, for the remainder of my stay, I eagerly returned to that happy hour, savoring the flowing cocktails and every bite of that incredible guacamole. This is the closest recipe I have that emulates the wonderful flavors of that guacamole. The recipe is straightforward and easy to make.

Serves 4-6

4 ripe avocados
3/4 cup white onions, finely chopped
2 garlic cloves, minced
4 tablespoons fresh lime juice

3 tablespoons fresh cilantro, finely chopped
1/4 cup chopped radishes
1 1/4 teaspoon kosher salt

Cut the avocados in half lengthwise, remove the pits, and scoop the flesh into a bowl. Mash the avocados with a fork until they reach your desired consistency. Add the chopped onion, minced garlic, lime juice, chopped cilantro, and radishes to the bowl. Mix everything together until well combined. Taste the guacamole and more add salt as needed. Serve immediately with tortilla chips

Pimento Cheese

Preparing pimento cheese is an ode to simplicity, as each ingredient harmonizes effortlessly to create a timeless classic, making it a cherished part of the Southern culinary heritage. It is closely associated with Southern food traditions, social gatherings, picnics, and family meals. Living in Atlanta has given me a newfound appreciation for the many variations of pimento cheese. Whether you spread it on a burger, sandwich it between two slices of bread, or enjoy it as a dip with crackers, pimento cheese is a testament to the beauty of uncomplicated yet flavorful recipes.

Serves 4-6

8 ounces sharp cheddar cheese, freshly shredded
4 ounces Monterey Jack cheese, freshly shredded
1/2 cup mayonnaise
1/4 cup cream cheese, softened
1/4 cup diced pimentos, drained
1/4 teaspoon garlic powder

1 tablespoon grated onion
1/2 teaspoon Dijon mustard
1/4 teaspoon hot sauce (optional)
1/4 teaspoon paprika
1/4 teaspoon kosher salt
1/4 teaspoon freshly ground black pepper

In a large bowl, combine the shredded cheddar and Monterey Jack cheese. In a separate bowl, mix together the mayonnaise and cream cheese until smooth. Add the diced pimentos, garlic powder, grated onion, mustard, hot sauce, paprika, salt, and pepper to the mixture and stir to combine. Add the mayonnaise mixture to the cheese and stir until the cheese is evenly coated. Serve with crackers or celery.

Note:

-To ensure that the cheese mixture doesn't become grainy or oily, it's important to use room temperature cream cheese and mayonnaise.

-It's also important to shred the cheese instead of using pre-shredded cheese, as pre-shredded cheese is coated in cellulose powder to prevent clumping, which can affect the texture of the final dish. To avoid this, shred the cheese yourself using a box grater or food processor.

Bacon-Wrapped Chorizo-Stuffed Dates

During my culinary school internship at a restaurant in Louisville, Kentucky, I learned to make these dates. The original recipe was quite lengthy, so I simplified it for easier preparation at home. The combination of smoky, savory, and sweet flavors in this dish creates a complex and well-rounded taste. The salty and spicy chorizo balances the sweetness of the dates, while the creaminess of the goat cheese and the smokiness of the bacon brings everything together. These dates make for an excellent make-ahead dish that can be easily reheated when guests arrive.

Serves 4-6

- **6 ounces raw chorizo, not cured**
- **15 Medjool dates, pitted**
- **3 ounces plain goat cheese, room temperature**
- **3 ounces cream cheese, room temperature**
- **15 pieces of bacon**
- **15 wooden toothpicks**
- **1 (24-ounce) jar store bought marinara sauce**
- **2 teaspoons smoked paprika**
- **2 ounces crumbled blue cheese**
- **3 scallions, minced**

Preheat oven to 400 degrees F.

Start by cooking the chorizo in a pan over medium heat for 5 to 8 minutes until fully cooked. Drain the chorizo and set it aside to cool. Once the chorizo has cooled, combine it in a bowl with the goat cheese and cream cheese. Take the dates and stuff them with the chorizo mixture, overstuffing them just a little. Next, wrap a piece of bacon around each date and secure it with a toothpick. Place the dates on a sheet tray lined with parchment paper and cook in the oven for 13 to 15 minutes, or until the bacon is crunchy. (Note: the chorizo is already cooked, so you only need to cook the bacon.)

To serve, heat the marinara sauce and 2 teaspoons of smoked paprika in a saucepan. Pour some of the sauce over the dates, and sprinkle blue cheese crumbles and scallions on top before serving.

Note:

- These can be made ahead 1 day and placed in a container in the refrigerator. To reheat them, place them in an oven preheated to 350 degrees F. Pull them out after 10 minutes or when they are hot in the center.

Baked Spinach and Artichoke Dip

It's believed that the dish originated in restaurants, particularly in California, where chefs began experimenting with new ways to use spinach and artichokes. While this recipe may not be the healthiest appetizer out there, it's definitely worth indulging in every once in a while. And the best part? It's incredibly easy to make. This dip is creamy, flavorful, and downright addictive.

-Serves 4-6

3 tablespoons dried onions
1 (10-ounce) package frozen spinach, thawed, chopped, and drained
1 (14-ounce) can artichoke hearts, drained and chopped
1 (8-ounce) package cream cheese, softened
1 cup mayonnaise
1 cup sour cream
2 garlic cloves, minced
1/4 teaspoon kosher salt
1/4 teaspoon black pepper
1/2 cup grated Parmesan cheese
2 teaspoons Worcestershire sauce
1 tablespoon chives, minced
tortilla chips for serving

Preheat oven to 350 degrees F.

Rehydrate the 3 tablespoons of dried onions with 2 to 3 tablespoons of water and set aside for 5 minutes.

In a large mixing bowl, combine the thawed and drained spinach, chopped artichoke hearts, cream cheese, mayonnaise, sour cream, minced garlic, salt, black pepper, Parmesan cheese, Worcestershire sauce, chives, and rehydrated onions. Mix well until all ingredients are evenly combined. Transfer the mixture to a 9x6-inch baking dish. Bake for 25 to 30 minutes, or until the top is golden brown and the dip is bubbly. Remove from the oven and let it cool for a few minutes.

Serve the dip warm with tortilla chips for dipping and a side of salsa.

Note:

- It's important to ensure that the spinach is drained well before adding it to the mixture to prevent excess moisture from making the dip too watery.

- The cream cheese should be softened to room temperature before mixing to ensure a smooth and even consistency.

- You can make this dip 1 day ahead and refrigerate it until ready to bake. Increase the baking time by 5 to 10 minutes if baking the dip straight from the refrigerator.

Caramelized Onion Dip

Growing up, my sister and I adored our go-to sour cream and dried onion soup mix dip. We were so proud of our creation. However, we've since discovered an unbeatable homemade version. Taking the time to caramelize onions from scratch is a step worth embracing, especially for memorable gatherings. The resulting dip boasts a rich and authentic flavor that never fails to impress a crowd.

Serves 4-6

Onions:
2 large onions, cut in half, sliced into 1/8-inch slices
4 tablespoons butter
2 tablespoons olive oil
1 tablespoon dried thyme
1 teaspoon kosher salt
2 teaspoon granulated white sugar

Dip:
1 (8-ounce) package cream cheese at room temperature
1/2 cup mayonnaise
1/2 cup sour cream
3/4 teaspoon garlic powder
1/4 teaspoon ground black pepper
1/2 teaspoon kosher salt
2 tablespoons Worcestershire sauce
3 teaspoons hot sauce
juice of half a lemon

Using a mandoline, cut the onions into 1/8-inch thick slices.

In a large sauté pan over medium fire, melt 4 tablespoons of butter with 2 tablespoons of olive oil. Add the onions, along with 1 tablespoon of dried thyme and 1 teaspoon of kosher salt. Cook the onions over low heat for approximately 45 to 60 minutes, stirring occasionally, until they are deeply caramelized and golden brown. Adjust the cooking time as needed to achieve the desired level of caramelization. Sprinkle the granulated white sugar over the caramelized onions and cook for an additional 5 minutes, stirring gently. Remove the pan from the heat and let the onions cool.

In a separate mixing bowl, combine cream cheese at room temperature, mayonnaise, sour cream, garlic powder, ground black pepper, kosher salt, Worcestershire sauce, hot sauce and lemon juice.

Once the onions have cooled, add them to the mixing bowl with the rest of the ingredients and stir well to combine. If the dip is too thick, add one tablespoon of hot water and stir until it reaches your desired consistency.

Serve the dip with kettle-style potato chips, as they can withstand the rigors of dipping without breaking. Alternatively, pretzels can also serve as a good dipping vehicle.

Note:

- For best results, make this dip a day or two ahead to allow the flavors to fully develop. This is because caramelizing the onions creates amino acids that contribute to a deeper, more complex flavor over time.

- Try slathering this on top of a juicy cheeseburger in place of mayonnaise.

Boursin Cheese and Pear Quesadilla

During my time living in Chicago, I frequently made this appetizer when pears were in season, from September through April. Marty and I enjoyed experimenting with different cheeses, using Camembert, Brie, or Gorgonzola, and occasionally substituting a drizzle of balsamic for the Dijon mustard. We have also tried using thinly sliced Pink Lady apples, which worked out great.

Serves 4-6

1 (12-ounce) package Garlic and Fine Herbs Boursin cheese
3 tablespoons Dijon mustard
8 (8-inch) flour tortillas
4 ripe Bosc pears, cored and thinly sliced

1/2 cup fresh grated Parmesan cheese
1/4 cup chopped fresh basil
3 tablespoons honey
3 tablespoons minced chives
olive oil
kosher salt, to taste

In a small bowl, mix together the cheese with the Dijon mustard until well combined. Lay one tortilla flat on a work surface and spread some of the cheese mixture (about 3 to 4 tablespoons) evenly over the tortilla. Arrange some of the sliced Bosc pears over the cheese mixture and sprinkle with some of the grated Parmesan cheese and basil. Drizzle 1 teaspoon of the honey with a spoon over the tops of the pears and sprinkle some chives. Top with another tortilla and press down lightly. Heat 1 tablespoon of olive oil in a large skillet over medium fire. Place the quesadilla in the skillet and cook for 2 to 3 minutes, until the bottom tortilla is golden brown and crispy. Carefully flip the quesadilla over and cook for an additional 2 to 3 minutes, until the second side is golden brown and the cheese is melted. Remove from the skillet and let cool for a minute before slicing into wedges. Sprinkle the tops of the sliced quesadilla with kosher salt and serve.

Note: Here are some variations and substitutions for this recipe.

- If you can't find Boursin cheese, mix some room temperature cream cheese with some Worcestershire sauce, thyme, and chives and proceed with the recipe.

- Instead of Boursin cheese, substitute Gorgonzola, Brie, or goat cheese.

- If Bosc pears are not available, substitute Anjou or use Honeycrisp or Pink Lady apples.

Easy Hummus

This hummus recipe is a true gem in the world of homemade dips. Its simplicity in preparation belies the complex and satisfying flavors it delivers. This shortcut proves that remarkable taste can still be achieved with a simple can from your pantry.

Serves 4-6

1 (15-ounce) can of chickpeas (garbanzo beans), drained and rinsed
1/4 cup tahini
1/4 cup extra virgin olive oil
3 cloves garlic, minced

2 tablespoons fresh lemon juice
1/2 teaspoon ground cumin
1/4 teaspoon of kosher salt
2 tablespoons of capers
Optional toppings: olive oil, paprika, chopped parsley

In a food processor or blender, combine the chickpeas, tahini, olive oil, minced garlic, lemon juice, cumin, and salt. Blend the ingredients until smooth. If the mixture is too thick, you can add a little water (start with 2 to 3 tablespoons) to achieve your desired consistency. Taste and adjust the seasoning by adding more salt or lemon juice if needed. Transfer the hummus to a serving bowl. Drizzle with a bit of olive oil, sprinkle with paprika, and garnish with chopped parsley, if desired. Serve with pita bread, fresh vegetables, or your favorite dipping items.

Grilled Elotes with Chipotle Cream and Cornbread Crumbs

This recipe takes regular grilled corn with butter and elevates it to something truly special. By grilling the corn with a spicy chipotle mayo and topping it with crunchy cornbread crumbs, this dish becomes a delightful celebration of the sweetness and flavor of fresh corn. It's perfect for summertime when the grill is a staple for outdoor gatherings and cookouts.

Serves 6

6 ears of corn, shucked

Cornbread Crumbs:
4 cups store bought or leftover cornbread
1 tablespoon butter

Chipotle Cream:
1/2 cup mayonnaise
1/4 cup sour cream
2 chipotle chiles from a can in adobo
1/2 teaspoon cumin powder
1 teaspoon garlic powder
2 tablespoons fresh lime juice
1/4 teaspoon kosher salt

Garnish:
3 tablespoons chives, chopped
1/4 cup cotija or crumbled feta (optional)

Preheat your grill to medium heat.

Cook corn: Bring a large pot of water to a boil, throw the corn in the pot, and cook for 4 to 5 minutes. Once cooked, remove them and set them aside.

Cornbread crumbs: In a sauté pan over medium heat put the butter and the corn bread. Break up the bread with a spoon and toast the bread crumbs for 3 to 4 minutes, then set aside. Make sure you break the corn bread so it resembles bread crumbs.

Chipotle cream: Add the ingredients for the chipotle cream to a bowl and use an immersion blender to puree the mixture.

Brush some of the chipotle cream over the corn and grill them for about 3 to 4 minutes until they are golden brown.

Remove the corn from the grill, slather some more chipotle cream over the corn, sprinkle chives, cotija cheese or crumbled feta, and cornbread crumbs on top. Enjoy immediately.

Crostini

These bite-sized flavor explosions atop toasted baguette slices embody both versatility and elegance, making them the ultimate appetizer choice for any occasion. With crostini, you have the freedom to unleash your creativity and wow your guests with a medley of enticing toppings. Don't hesitate to repurpose leftover ingredients from the previous night's dinner—crostini is the perfect canvas for culinary experimentation. What sets crostinis apart is their adaptability and make-ahead nature. This liberates you to fully immerse yourself in the joy of hosting, mingling with friends, and creating cherished memories, rather than being confined to the kitchen during the festivities. Below is the crostini recipe for the recipes that follow.

Crostini

Makes 20 crostini

1 baguette, cut into 1/4-inch slices
3/4 cup extra virgin olive oil

1 teaspoon kosher salt

Preheat oven to 350 degrees F.

Brush both sides of the bread with olive oil and arrange on a sheet pan lined with parchment paper. Sprinkle the tops with the 1 teaspoon of kosher salt and bake for 5 to 8 minutes or until they have a crispy exterior. Remove from the pan and allow to cool.

Assemble: Put about 1/2 tablespoon of topping on a crostini and sprinkle it with some of the chives. Add some salt on top of the crostini if you find the crostini needs it. Let this come to room temperature before serving.

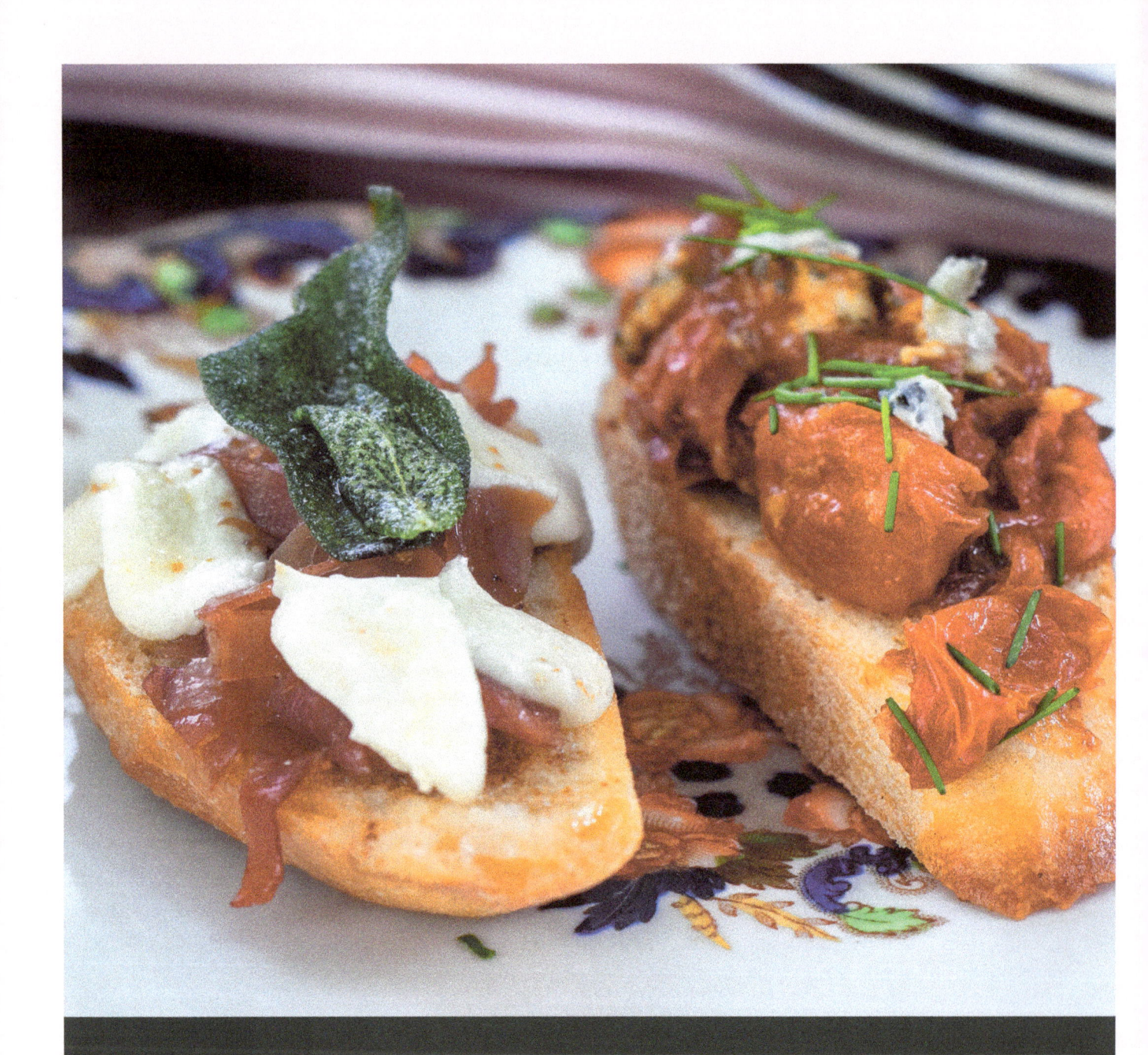

Blistered Tomato and Blue Cheese Bruschetta

This dish features blistered cherry tomatoes mixed with tangy blue cheese on top of crispy crostini. The tomatoes are roasted and deglazed with balsamic vinegar to create a rich and complex flavor profile. The caramelization from roasting adds depth of flavor and sweetness to the tomatoes, while the blue cheese brings a tangy and creamy element to the dish.

Serves 4-6

Roast Tomatoes:
2 pints cherry tomatoes, cut in half
1/2 teaspoon kosher salt
1 teaspoon granulated white sugar
3 tablespoons Worcestershire sauce
1 teaspoon dried thyme
3 tablespoons olive oil
2 tablespoons balsamic vinegar
2 tablespoons fresh lemon juice
6 ounces blue cheese
Crostini recipe is on page 43

Preheat oven to 375 degrees F.

Roast Tomatoes:

First toss the halved cherry tomatoes in a bowl with the kosher salt, sugar, Worcestershire sauce, dried thyme and olive oil. Then place the mixture in a single layer on a sheet pan lined with parchment paper. Roast in the oven at 375 degrees F for 35 to 40 minutes, stirring every 10 to 15 minutes for even cooking. After roasting, deglaze the pan with balsamic vinegar and lemon juice, using a spatula to scrape up any caramelized bits. Transfer the tomato mixture to a bowl and let cool. Once it has cooled, mix in the blue cheese, using a spatula to combine thoroughly.

Spread a tablespoon of the tomato mixture onto the crostini and serve.

Note: Here are some variations you can make for this recipe.

- Swap out the blue cheese for feta or goat cheese for a different flavor.

- Add a pinch of red pepper flakes for some heat.

- Top the finished bruschetta with fresh herbs, like basil or parsley, for a pop of freshness.

Prosciutto, Mozzarella, and Sage Brown Butter Crostini

These bite-sized toasts can be assembled in advance, making them a great option for entertaining. The crispy bread provides a sturdy base for the layers of thinly sliced prosciutto and melted mozzarella, while the sage brown butter adds a depth of flavor. The combination of savory and earthy flavors in this dish is a true testament to the art of simple but delicious cooking. Fire up the oven, break out the butter, and get ready to indulge in some seriously tasty crostini.

Serves 4-6

Sage Brown Butter:
8 tablespoons (1 stick) unsalted butter
9-10 sage leaves, minced
zest of 1 lemon

Crostini:
1 baguette, cut into 18-20 1/4-inch slices
8 ounces prosciutto, sliced thinly (about 14 slices) and minced
8 ounces fresh mozzarella cheese
2 tablespoons chives, minced
kosher salt and black pepper

Preheat oven to 375 degrees F.

Sage brown butter: Melt the butter over medium heat, stirring occasionally with a heat-resistant spatula or wooden spoon. The butter will start to foam and sizzle. Continue cooking the butter, swirling the pan occasionally to ensure even heat distribution. As the water content evaporates from the butter, it will begin to turn golden brown. Keep a close eye on the butter as it browns. You'll notice a nutty aroma and small brown specks forming at the bottom of the pan. This is an indication that the milk solids in the butter are caramelizing. Remove the pan from the heat and add the minced sage leaves and lemon zest to the brown butter, stirring to combine. Set aside.

Crostini: Next, line a half-sheet pan with parchment paper. Place 1/2 tablespoon of prosciutto over the top of each crostini, followed by torn pieces of mozzarella. Arrange the crostini on the sheet pan and bake in the oven for 8 to 10 minutes, or until the mozzarella is melted and the bread is toasted.

Remove from the oven and spoon the sage brown butter over each crostini, making sure to use the brown bits at the bottom of the pan. Sprinkle with minced chives, kosher salt, and black pepper, then serve warm or at room temperature.

Note:

- It's important to closely monitor the process of making brown butter to prevent burning. The butter can go from perfectly browned to burnt in a matter of seconds.

- The brown butter can be made up to a day in advance; simply cover it and refrigerate until ready to use.

- You can also assemble the crostini up to two hours before your guests arrive, without cooking them. Then, when your guests arrive, warm up the brown butter, pop the crostini in the oven, and continue with the recipe.

Lunch

Lunch, often overshadowed in the hustle and bustle of our busy lives, holds a special place in our day that deserves to be celebrated with elegance. While the concept of lunch has become increasingly casual over the past few decades, there is no reason why this midday meal cannot be a moment of refinement and delight.

In the world of lunchtime cuisine, sandwiches reign supreme, offering a harmonious balance of convenience and flavor. Classic options, like egg and BLT sandwiches, have stood the test of time for good reason. With their simple yet satisfying combinations, they provide a quick and delightful respite from the demands of the day. However, lunch is not limited to sandwiches alone.

Soups and salads have also become synonymous with the midday meal, offering a world of possibilities for creativity and nourishment. A well-crafted soup warms the soul and tantalizes the taste buds, providing comfort and sustenance in a single bowl.

Salads, on the other hand, bring freshness, vibrancy, and nutritional balance to the lunchtime table. They serve as a canvas for culinary exploration, allowing you to play with an array of ingredients, dressings, and textures. Whether you prefer a crisp garden salad or a robust protein-packed creation, salads offer versatility and the opportunity to customize to your heart's content.

Sandwiches

BLTs with Roasted Tomato and Garlic Mayonnaise

One summer in Key West, I fondly remember surprising my parents, husband, and sister with platters of crispy bacon, toasted bread, roasted cherry tomatoes, and a selection of salad greens all destined to create mouthwatering BLT sandwiches. As I proudly announced that lunch was served, my sister's first bite prompted an exclamation that these were, without a doubt, the finest BLTs she had ever tasted. To make BLTs, I roasted the cherry tomatoes, intensifying their tomatoey flavor and acidity, so they would play well with the smoke and fat from the bacon. Then, I added garlic and lemon juice to the mayo to create a tangy, flavorful aioli that would complement the other ingredients. The result was a sandwich that was bursting with flavor, with the perfect balance of salty, sweet, tangy, and smoky. It's the ultimate comfort food, perfect for a lazy day with family.

Makes 4 sandwiches

Roasted Tomatoes:
1 pint cherry tomatoes, cut in half
1/2 teaspoon kosher salt
1 teaspoon white sugar
1 1/2 tablespoon of Worcestershire sauce
1/2 teaspoon dried thyme
1 tablespoon olive oil
1 tablespoon balsamic vinegar

Garlic Mayo:
1 cup of mayonnaise
3 cloves garlic, finely grated with a microplane or zester
1 tablespoon lemon juice

Bacon:
8 slices of thick-cut bacon

Bread:
8 slices of sourdough bread, toasted

1 head of butter lettuce

Preheat oven to 375 degrees F.

Roasted tomatoes: On a sheet pan lined with parchment paper, mix together the cherry tomatoes, salt, sugar, Worcestershire sauce, thyme, and olive oil. Place the tomatoes in a single layer on the sheet pan. Bake for 25 minutes, then use a spatula to toss the tomatoes and spread them out again. Bake for an additional 10 to 15 minutes, until the tomatoes are caramelized and soft. Remove the tomatoes from the oven and deglaze the pan with balsamic vinegar. Scrape the tomatoes and any caramelized bits into a bowl and mash with a fork to make a spread. Set this aside.

Garlic mayo: Mix together the mayonnaise and garlic zest, along with lemon juice, salt, and pepper.

Bacon: Preheat the oven to 400 degrees F.

Place the bacon flat on a sheet pan lined with parchment paper. Cook the bacon for 15 to 18 minutes until crispy. Remove the bacon from the pan and set to drain on a plate lined with a paper towel. Save the bacon oil for cooking later in the week.

Assemble the sandwiches: Spread 1 tablespoon of garlic mayo on one side of each slice of bread. Take one slice of bread and top it with a layer of roasted tomatoes (about 1 to 2 tablespoons), followed by 2 to 3 slices of bacon, and a few leaves of butter lettuce. Top with another slice of bread, garlic mayo side down. Repeat with the remaining slices of bread and ingredients to make a total of 4 BLT sandwiches.

Egg Salad Sandwich

When it comes to egg salad, this recipe is my go-to choice. Its perfect mayonnaise-to-egg ratio, delightful texture, and straightforward flavors never fail to impress. The creamy goodness of the egg salad, complemented by the tangy grainy mustard and the refreshing taste of chives, makes for a truly mouthwatering sandwich. I highly recommend serving it on toasted bread, and if you're feeling adventurous, adding thinly sliced radishes for an extra kick. Trust me, it's an option worth considering!

Serves 6-8

Eggs:
16 eggs
Mayonnaise Mixture:
2 cups mayonnaise
1 small red onion, finely chopped
2 stalks celery, finely chopped
1 teaspoon kosher salt
3 teaspoon whole grain mustard
juice of 1 lemon or lime

2 garlic cloves, grated on a microplane
1/2 teaspoon black pepper
2 tablespoons fresh dill, chopped
4 scallions minced, green and white parts
Garnish:
4-6 radishes, thinly sliced on a mandoline (optional)

Boil the eggs: To boil the eggs, place them in a pot, and cover them completely with water from the tap, leaving about 1 inch of water above the eggs. Bring the water to a boil, then remove the pot from the fire and cover it with a lid. Set a timer for 10 minutes. After 10 minutes, drain the hot water from the pot and shake it gently to crack the eggshells. Fill the pot with cold tap water and let the eggs sit in the water for about 2 minutes before peeling them.

To peel the eggs, crack one on its side and roll it gently on the counter to loosen the shell. Peel the shell from the egg and roughly chop the egg on a cutting board.

Egg salad: To a large bowl, add the ingredients for the mayonnaise mixture and mix until combined.

Fold the chopped eggs into the mayonnaise mixture. (If the mixture is too dry, add 1 tablespoon of mayonnaise.) Taste it and add more salt if needed.

Serve with some toasted whole grain bread and some thinly sliced radishes (if using) on top of the egg salad.

Note:

- In the directions, I employ a unique technique when boiling the eggs: bringing them to a boil and immediately turning off the heat. This approach is intentional, designed to avoid prolonged boiling. The reason behind this method lies in chemistry. Boiling eggs for an extended period can trigger a reaction between the iron present in the yolks and the sulfur in the whites, resulting in the formation of iron sulfide compounds. While this chemical reaction is harmless from a safety perspective, it can lead to the yolks taking on a greenish or grayish hue, which is less appealing when our goal is to achieve vibrant, bright yellow cooked yolks. This technique ensures that the eggs are perfectly cooked without compromising their visual appeal.are avoiding boiling the eggs in water because it triggers a reaction between the iron in the yolks and the sulfur in the whites, forming iron sulfide compounds. This reaction causes the yolks to turn greenish or grayish in color, which is harmless but undesirable if we aim for a vibrant, bright yellow cooked yolk.

- Mixing the mayonnaise ingredients together first ensures that they are evenly distributed throughout the egg salad, allowing the flavors to meld together and creating a harmonious taste experience.

- You can make this egg salad 4 days ahead, but don't mix the radishes into the egg mixture. It can be kept covered in the refrigerator for 4 days.

Chicken Pesto Sandwiches

In my twenties, I recall the widespread popularity of pesto, which found its way onto sandwiches, meat entrees, and numerous pasta dishes. Fast forward to today, and chicken pesto sandwiches remain a fantastic choice for make-ahead meals, particularly for a bagged lunch, BBQs, or picnics. Preparing the pesto in advance allows the flavors to harmonize and intensify, resulting in an exceptionally delightful eating experience.

Serves 4

4 boneless, skinless chicken breasts
kosher salt and black pepper
8 slices of thick, crusty bread
8 tablespoons store bought pesto sauce (or use recipe below)
8 slices of tomatoes
8 romaine leaves

Chicken: Rub the chicken breasts with some olive oil and sprinkle some salt and pepper over them. Place the chicken on a sheet pan lined with parchment paper and cook them in the oven for 25 to 30 minutes. The chicken should reach an internal temperature of 165 degrees F. Allow the chicken to cool.

Take a slice of thick, crusty bread and spread about a tablespoon or two of pesto sauce on the bottom half of the slice. Place two slices of tomato on top of the pesto, then the chicken, then the romaine leaves. Do these steps to the remaining sandwiches. If you want to make the pesto instead of using store bought, here is the recipe for pesto.

Basic Pesto

2 cups fresh basil leaves
1/2 cup grated Parmesan cheese
1/2 cup walnuts or pine nuts
3 garlic cloves
1/2 cup extra virgin olive oil
1/2 teaspoon kosher salt
1/2 teaspoon freshly ground black pepper

In a food processor or blender, combine the fresh basil leaves, grated Parmesan cheese, walnuts or pine nuts, garlic cloves, salt, and pepper. Pulse the ingredients a few times to break them down. Gradually pour in the extra virgin olive oil while the food processor is running.

Continue blending until the mixture becomes a smooth and creamy paste. Taste the pesto and adjust the seasoning as desired, adding more salt and pepper if needed.

Notes:

- Cooking the chicken breasts to an internal temperature of 165 degrees F ensures they are thoroughly cooked and safe to eat. This temperature is considered the minimum safe internal temperature for poultry, eliminating any potential risks of foodborne illnesses.

- If you have leftover pesto, store it in an airtight container in the refrigerator. To prevent oxidation and allow it to maintain its vibrant green color, drizzle a thin layer of olive oil over the top of the pesto before sealing the container.

- Don't be afraid to experiment with different herbs and nuts in your pesto. While basil and pine nuts are traditional, you can try variations like cilantro and cashews or arugula and almonds for unique flavor profiles.

Soups

Carrot, Orange, and Ginger Soup

Carrot juice and orange juice are a common pairing found in smoothies and juices at local supermarkets. Why not make a soup with this delicious combination? The sweet earthiness of the carrots and the bright acidity of the oranges make this soup burst with flavor. It can be served warm during the fall and winter months, or chilled during the summer.

Serves 4-6

4 tablespoons butter
1 tablespoon olive oil
2 large yellow onions, chopped
2 teaspoons dried thyme
2 teaspoons dried tarragon
2 tablespoons grated ginger
2 garlic cloves, minced
2 pounds carrots, peeled and chopped

32 ounces chicken stock
4 tablespoons freshly grated ginger
2 teaspoons cumin powder
10 ounces orange juice
6 ounces heavy cream
2 teaspoons black pepper
2 teaspoons kosher salt

Garnish:

1 teaspoon orange zest (after zesting, use the juice from the orange in the soup)

3 tablespoons chives, minced
4 ounces heavy cream

In a medium stock pot over medium heat, melt the butter with the olive oil. Add the chopped onions, dried thyme, dried tarragon, and grated ginger. Cook for 15 to 20 minutes. Add the minced garlic and cook for an additional minute. Add the chopped carrots and 24 ounces of chicken stock. Bring the mixture to a boil, then reduce the fire and simmer for about 25 minutes or until the carrots are easily pierced with a fork.

Using a slotted spoon, remove the carrots and onions from the pot and place them in a food processor or blender. Add 1/4 cup of the remaining chicken stock and puree the mixture until smooth. If needed, you can add more stock to the food processor to aid in the pureeing process. Return the pureed mixture to the pot and add the remaining chicken stock, grated ginger, cumin powder, and orange juice. Bring the mixture to a boil and let it cook for 1 minute. Then, reduce the heat and stir in the heavy cream, black pepper, and kosher salt. Allow the soup to simmer for 5 minutes.

If the soup is too thick for your taste, add additional chicken stock to achieve your desired consistency.

When ready to serve, stir in the orange zest and top with minced chives. Drizzle a tablespoon of the cream over the top of the soup. Serve with crusty bread.

Note:

- If you prefer a thicker soup, you can reduce the amount of chicken stock or increase the amount of carrots.

- To make this soup vegetarian or vegan, substitute the chicken stock with vegetable stock and replace the butter and cream with a plant-based alternative.

- Leftover soup can be stored in an airtight container in the refrigerator for up to 5 days, or frozen for up to 3 months.

- When reheating, add a little bit of stock or water to thin out the soup as it may thicken in the fridge or freezer.

Onion Soup

Onion soup holds a special place in culinary history, tracing its origins back to ancient times when onions were considered a staple ingredient due to their long shelf life. France has popularized onion soup and elevated it to a beloved classic, particularly the version known as French Onion Soup. The French have perfected the art of caramelizing onions to create a rich and flavorful base, making their version of onion soup iconic worldwide. Not all onion soups are created equal, and this recipe stands out as truly exceptional. It's worth giving it a try for the unparalleled flavors it delivers. The secret lies in properly caramelizing the onions to coax out their inherent sweetness, resulting in a soup that is truly sublime.

Serves 4-6

1 (4-ounce) stick unsalted butter
6 slices bacon, cut into lardons (matchsticks)
4 large red onions, sliced into 1/4-inch slices
4 white onions, sliced into 1/4-inch slices
2 tablespoons dried thyme
1 teaspoon granulated white sugar

4 tablespoons balsamic vinegar
8 ounces Cognac
4 garlic cloves, minced
8 ounces white wine
32 ounces beef stock
1 teaspoon kosher salt
1 teaspoon black pepper
10 slices baguette bread, toasted
10 ounces Gruyere cheese, grated

In a stockpot over medium heat, melt the butter. Add the bacon and cook until crispy, about 8 to 10 minutes. Using a slotted spoon, remove the bacon and set it aside. Add the sliced onions and thyme to the pot and cook for about 45 to 60 minutes, stirring occasionally, or until the onions are evenly dark in color. Add the sugar to the pot and cook for an additional 2 minutes. Deglaze the pan with balsamic vinegar and Cognac. Cook and stir for 2 to 3 minutes, scraping the dark bits from the bottom of the pan. Add minced garlic and cook for 3 to 4 minutes. Pour in the white wine, beef stock, salt, and pepper. Bring the mixture to a boil for 3 minutes, then simmer uncovered for 40 minutes.

When you are ready to serve, ladle the soup into bowls and add one or two slices of toasted baguette. Finish with the grated cheese and some of the reserved bacon.

Note:

- Make sure to slice the onions evenly and thinly to ensure even cooking and flavor distribution.

- Deglazing the pan with balsamic vinegar, and Cognac adds depth and complexity to the soup.

- Leftover soup can be stored in an airtight container in the refrigerator for up to 3 to 4 days or frozen for up to 3 months.

Roasted Vegetable Soup

Vegetable soups are often made with canned ingredients for convenience, but I find that taking the time to roast fresh vegetables in the oven is a simple way to intensify their flavors and create a rich depth of flavor. This soup features a variety of fresh vegetables, including mushrooms, red onion, carrots, sweet potatoes, and Yukon Gold potatoes, seasoned with rosemary, thyme, salt, and pepper. After roasting, the vegetables are blended with chicken stock and chopped tomatoes to create a smooth, hearty soup.

Serves 4-6

Roast Vegetables:
4 garlic cloves, minced
16 ounces white mushrooms, sliced into 1/4-inch pieces
1 large red onion, sliced into 1/2-inch pieces
1 pound carrots, peeled, cut into 1-inch pieces
2 sweet potatoes, peeled, cut into 1-inch pieces
3 Yukon Gold potatoes, peeled, cut into 1-inch pieces

1 tablespoon rosemary, chopped
1 tablespoon thyme, chopped
1/4 cup olive oil
1 1/2 teaspoons kosher salt
1 teaspoon black pepper

Soup:
24-32 ounces chicken stock
1 (15-ounce) can chopped tomatoes, drained
1/4 cup chives, chopped

Preheat oven to 425 degrees F.

Roast vegetables: Put all the vegetables on a sheet pan lined with parchment paper, and toss them with the rosemary, thyme, olive oil, salt, and pepper. Spread them out in a single layer to ensure even cooking.

Roast in the oven for 25 minutes, then toss them and spread them out again before returning them to the oven. Continue to cook for another 15 minutes, or until the vegetables are tender enough to be easily pierced with a fork.

Soup: Add the roasted vegetables and drained tomatoes to a food processor along with 24 ounces of stock. Pulse the mixture until it becomes a smooth puree, then transfer it to a stock pot. Bring the soup to a boil, then reduce the fire to medium. If the soup is too thick, add a little more stock to thin it out. Let the soup simmer for 20 minutes.

Serve with chopped chives and toasted bread.

Note:

- Roast the vegetables properly. Roasting the vegetables in the oven is what gives this soup its depth of flavor. Make sure to spread the vegetables out in a single layer on the sheet pan so they roast evenly. If the vegetables are too crowded, they may steam instead of roast, resulting in a less flavorful soup.

- Leftover soup can be stored in an airtight container in the refrigerator for up to 3 to 4 days or frozen for up to 3 months. When reheating, add a little bit of stock or water to thin out the soup as it may thicken in the fridge or freezer.

Salads

Cucumber and Radish Salad with Red Onion and Dill

During the hot summer months at our farm, it was essential to have a refreshing and easy-to-make salad on hand. This cucumber, radish, and dill salad was the perfect solution. This was made ahead of time, so it could be chilled in the fridge and enjoyed without heating up the kitchen. This salad was a lifesaver during the scorching hot months of July and August.

Serves 4

2 large English cucumbers, thinly sliced
1/2 red onion, thinly sliced
1 cup radishes, thinly sliced
1 cup sour cream
3 tablespoons fresh dill, chopped

2 tablespoons fresh parsley, chopped
2 tablespoons white wine vinegar
1 tablespoon sugar
1 teaspoon kosher salt
1/2 teaspoon black pepper

In a large mixing bowl, combine the sour cream, chopped dill, parsley, white vinegar, sugar, salt, and pepper. Mix well until the dressing is smooth and well combined. Add the sliced cucumbers, radishes, and red onions to the bowl with the dressing. Toss gently to coat the vegetables evenly with the dressing. Let the salad marinate in the refrigerator for at least 30 minutes to allow the flavors to meld together. You can also refrigerate it for longer if desired. Before serving, taste and adjust the seasoning if needed. You can add more salt, pepper, or vinegar according to your preference. Serve the cucumber and radish salad chilled as a refreshing side dish with grilled meats or as part of a light summer meal.

Note:

- The longer the salad sits in the fridge, the more flavorful it becomes, so feel free to make it ahead of time and store it in an airtight container for up to 2 days.

- If you prefer a lighter version, you can omit the sour cream and use Greek yogurt or a light vinaigrette as a dressing alternative.

- To make the salad more filling, you can add some cooked quinoa, chickpeas, or grilled chicken on top.

- Feel free to add feta cheese, goat cheese, or shaved Parmesan to change the salad's flavor.

- Feel free to add some fresh basil or mint leaves to enhance the flavor profile.

Wedge Salad with Blue Cheese, Bacon, and Tomatoes

When I was younger, I used to go to steakhouses where a part of the first course was an iceberg wedge salad with crumbled bacon, sliced tomatoes, and creamy blue cheese dressing. Although some chefs have moved away from using iceberg lettuce, I still enjoy this salad very much. I love the crunchiness of the lettuce and the convenience of being able to prepare everything beforehand and compose the salad when it is time to eat.

Serves 4

Bacon:
10 slices thick-cut bacon

Dressing:
4 ounces blue cheese
2/3 cup milk
3/4 cup mayonnaise
2 tablespoons white vinegar
2 teaspoons garlic powder
1/2 cup sour cream
1 teaspoon kosher salt
5 scallions, chopped, both green and white parts

Salad:
1 head iceberg lettuce, cut into quarters
4 ounces blue cheese
1 small red onion, cut in half and sliced thinly
2 cups cherry tomatoes, sliced in half

Preheat oven 400 degrees F.

Put 4 plates into your freezer and pull them out when you are ready to plate the salad.

Bacon: On a sheet pan lined with parchment paper, place the bacon and cook it in the oven for 12 to 16 minutes until the bacon is crispy. When the bacon has cooled, chop up the bacon and set it aside on a plate lined with a paper towel. (Save the bacon oil for cooking later in the week.)

Blue cheese dressing: Put the ingredients for the dressing into a bowl and whisk them together.

Salad: Put a wedge on each frozen plate. Ladle the blue cheese dressing over each iceberg wedge. Take the 4 ounces of blue cheese and crumble it over the wedges of lettuce. Do the same with the bacon, tomatoes and thinly sliced red onion.

Note:

- Adjust the consistency of the blue cheese dressing to your liking. If you prefer a thicker dressing, reduce the amount of milk slightly. If you prefer a thinner dressing, add a little more milk.

- To ensure even slicing of the red onion and cherry tomatoes, you can use a sharp knife or a mandoline slicer. This helps create uniform pieces that distribute the flavors evenly throughout the salad.

Shaved Fennel with Onion and Torn Bread Croutons

Raw, shaved fennel and red onion make a great pairing because the fennel adds a subtle hint of anise and a pleasant depth of flavor, while the red onion adds a sharp, slightly sweet flavor. The addition of mint provides a refreshing and herbaceous note to this summery salad. With its super fresh, crunchy texture and ease of preparation, this salad is sure to become your go-to salad during hot summer months.

Serves 2-4

Croutons:
2 cups torn sourdough bread
3 tablespoons olive for the bread

Vinaigrette:
1 orange
2 tablespoons balsamic vinegar
1 tablespoon honey
1 teaspoon Dijon mustard
1 garlic clove, grated
4 tablespoons chives, chopped
1/4 teaspoon kosher salt
4 tablespoons mint, chopped
1/4 cup extra virgin olive oil

Salad:
2 fennel bulbs with the fronds
1/2 small red onion
4 ounces grated
Parmesan cheese

Preheat oven to 400 degrees F.

Croutons: Place the torn sourdough bread on a sheet pan lined with parchment paper. Drizzle 3 tablespoons of olive oil over the bread and toss to coat. Roast in a preheated oven at 400 degrees F for 6 to 8 minutes, or until the bread is toasted. Remove from the oven and set aside.

Vinaigrette: Begin by zesting two teaspoons of orange zest into a bowl. Next, juice the orange and pour the juice into the same bowl. Add the balsamic vinegar, honey, Dijon mustard, grated garlic, chopped chives, kosher salt, and chopped mint. Slowly pour the extra virgin olive oil into the bowl while whisking the mixture until it becomes emulsified. Taste the vinaigrette and adjust the seasoning if needed by adding more salt or acid. If the vinaigrette is too tart, you can add a bit more honey to balance the flavors.

Salad: To prepare the fennel, start by cutting off a thin slice from the bottom and discard it. Then, cut off the fronds and set them aside for later use as a garnish. Use a mandoline to thinly shave the fennel and toss it in the vinaigrette. Next, remove the root from the half onion and use the mandoline to shave it thinly as well. Add the red onion to the vinaigrette and toss gently. Serve the salad with the sourdough croutons, fennel fronds, and grated Parmesan cheese.

Note:

- You can leave the fennel in the vinaigrette for 2 to 3 hours in the refrigerator and then serve it when your guests arrive. The flavors meld beautifully.

- The vinaigrette can be made ahead of time and stored in the refrigerator for up to 3 days.

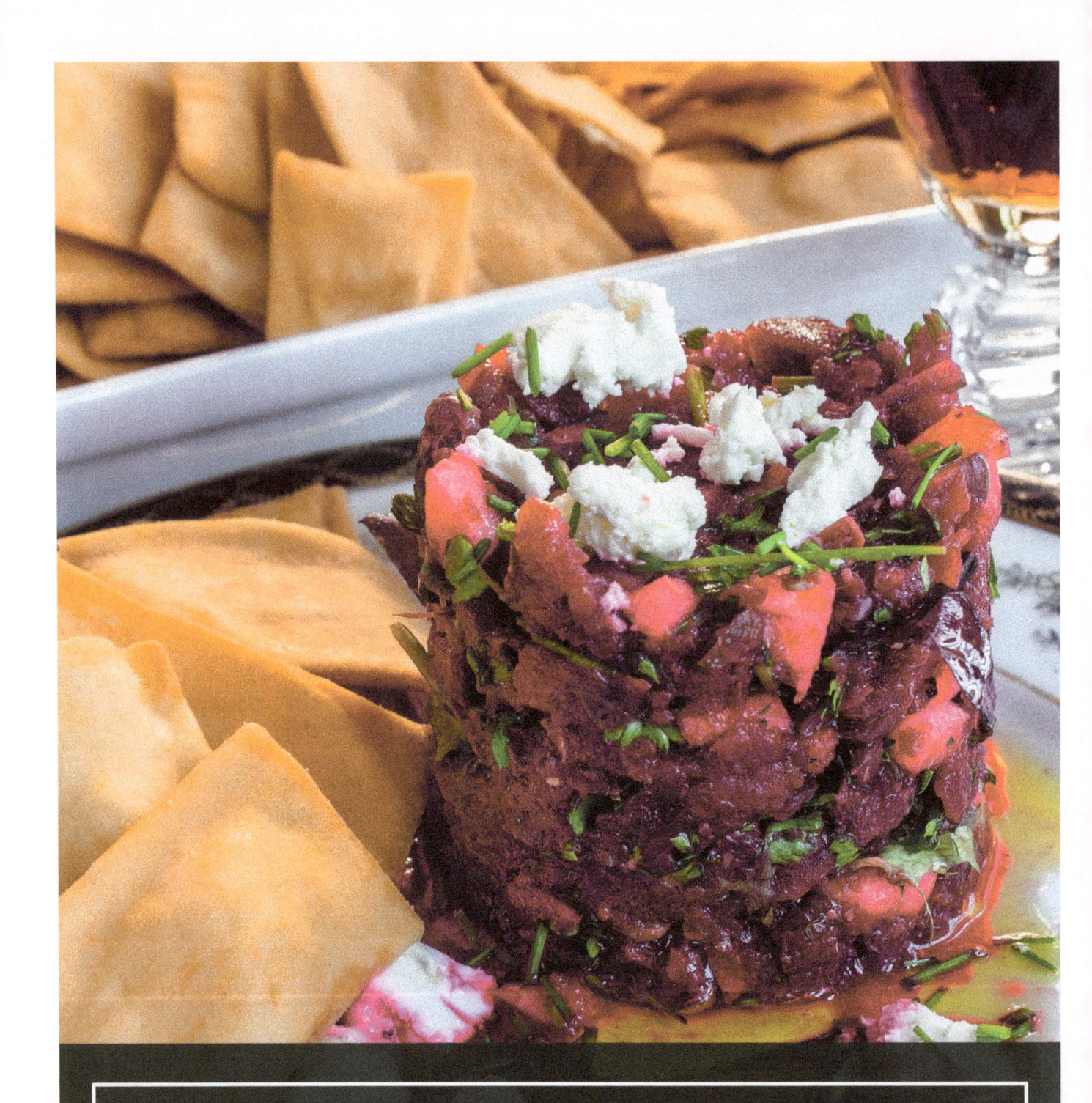

Beet Tartare

The recipe for Beet Tartare is not just a visually appealing vegetarian starter that incorporates classic elements of beef tartare, but it can also double as a fulfilling dinner main course. The beets' vivid red hues imitate the appearance of the meat dish, and the flavors are refreshing and harmonious. The dish is a feast for the eyes, and the presentation is exquisite.

Serves 4-6

Beets:
4 medium beets
3 tablespoon olive oil
1 tablespoon capers, finely chopped
1 tablespoon red onions, finely chopped
1 tablespoon Dijon mustard
1 tablespoon extra virgin olive oil
1 teaspoon apple cider vinegar
3 teaspoons soy sauce
1 teaspoon sriracha
2 garlic cloves, minced
1 tablespoon fresh parsley, finely chopped
1 Granny Smith apple, peeled and diced
2 tablespoons mayonnaise
1/2 teaspoon kosher salt

Greens:
1 cup baby spring mix
1 cup crumbled goat cheese
3 tablespoons chives, minced

Preheat oven to 400 degrees F.

Beet tartare: Rub the beets with 3 tablespoons of olive oil then wrap beets tightly in foil. Roast for 45 to 60 minutes, or until tender. Allow beets to cool completely; remove the skins. Cut the beets into smaller pieces that will fit into your food processor. Throw the beets into the food processor along with the capers, red onion, Dijon, 1 tablespoon of olive oil, apple cider vinegar, soy sauce, sriracha, and garlic cloves. Pulse the food processor a few times until the beets are chopped into small, uniform pieces. Remove the beet mixture and put it in a bowl. Throw in the parsley, apple, mayonnaise, and salt. Gently toss to incorporate the ingredients, especially the mayonnaise.

Plating: Put a round mold in the center of the plate. With your hands put some of the spring greens into the mold, then fill with the beet mixture and press down lightly. Remove the mold and sprinkle some of the goat cheese and chives over the beets. Serve with some crostini.

Note:

- When roasting the beets, make sure to wrap them tightly in foil to prevent any juices from leaking out. This will help ensure that the beets stay moist and tender.

- The use of a food processor is optional, as you can also finely chop the beets, capers, and onion by hand if you prefer. Just make sure to chop everything into small, uniform pieces.

- Make sure to use a round mold that is sturdy enough to hold the shape of the beet mixture. You can also use a biscuit cutter or other round object if you don't have a mold on hand.

Sides and Vegetables

Sides and vegetables, often overshadowed by their protein counterparts, possess an extraordinary ability to transform a meal into an unforgettable culinary experience. These culinary gems not only enhance and balance the flavors on the plate but also allow us to showcase the bountiful produce of each season, embracing the freshness and vibrancy of local ingredients.

Among the array of delightful options, dishes like the roasted carrots with cumin, ginger, and goat cheese exemplify the art of creating harmonious flavor profiles. The earthy sweetness of the roasted carrots, infused with the warm and aromatic notes of cumin and ginger, forms a symphony of tastes that beautifully complements a variety of main dishes. To add a touch of indulgence, a sprinkling of tangy and creamy goat cheese elevates each bite to new heights of luxury.

Similarly, the comforting appeal of braised Brussels sprouts demonstrates the remarkable potential of vegetables. Through the gentle and patient braising process, these humble sprouts are transformed into tender morsels of flavor. Enhanced with aromatic herbs, garlic, and a delicate acidity, they become a savory side dish that harmonizes with any meal. Their nuanced taste, delicately balancing bitterness and richness, adds depth and character to the dining experience.

Sides and vegetables play both leading and supporting roles, continuously inspiring me in the kitchen. A well-paired side or vegetable can effortlessly elevate a simple whole roasted chicken or a braised lamb shank to new heights.

Whether they serve as the star of the show or provide the supporting act, their versatility and adaptability never cease to inspire me. Each dish becomes an opportunity to explore new flavor combinations, techniques, and presentations, allowing me to express my culinary artistry and share my passion with those I cook for.

Roasted Carrots with Cumin, Ginger, and Goat Cheese

Roasted carrots are a simple and delicious side dish that pairs well with any meal. In this recipe, the warm and earthy flavors of cumin and cinnamon are complemented by the tangy and creamy goat cheese, creating a perfect balance of flavors. The addition of fresh lemon juice and grated ginger to the garlic butter sauce gives the dish a bright, zesty, and slightly spicy twist. This dish is easy to prepare and is a great way to showcase the natural sweetness of carrots.

Serves 4-6

3 pounds carrots, peeled and cut on the bias into 1-inch pieces
3 tablespoon olive oil
3 teaspoons ground cumin
2 teaspoons ground cinnamon
3 teaspoons kosher salt
3 tablespoons fresh thyme, chopped
4 garlic cloves, minced

4 tablespoons butter
1 tablespoon fresh lemon juice
1 tablespoon fresh ginger, grated
2-3 ounces goat cheese, crumbled
1/4 cup parsley, chopped
1/4 cup almonds, chopped (optional)

Preheat oven to 400 degrees F.

On a parchment covered sheet pan, put the carrots, olive oil, cumin, cinnamon, kosher salt, and thyme and toss together until combined. Spread the vegetables evenly around the sheet pan. Roast for 45 to 60 minutes or until the carrots yield to the tip of a knife.

While the carrots are cooking, put the butter in a small saucepan and melt the butter over medium fire, then add the garlic and cook for 1 minute. Add the lemon juice and grated ginger and stir. Cook for 2 more minutes, then set the garlic butter to the side.

Take the roasted cumin carrots out of the oven and put them in a serving dish. Pour the garlic butter over the carrots, crumble the goat cheese on top, and sprinkle the dish with parsley. If you are using almonds, toss them over the top of the carrots.

Note:

- Make sure to cut the carrots the same size to ensure they cook evenly.

- You can also adjust the amount of cumin and cinnamon to your preference, and experiment with other herbs or spices such as smoked paprika, coriander, or ginger for added depth of flavor.

- This dish is best served warm, but can be stored in an airtight container in the refrigerator for up to 3 days. When reheating, heat in the oven at 200 degrees F for 25 minutes, then sprinkle some fresh parsley and goat cheese on top for a pop of freshness.

Hasselback Potatoes with Rosemary and Parmesan

These crispy and savory potatoes are a beloved classic, originating in Sweden in the seventeenth century. The dish is named after the Hasselbacken Hotel in Stockholm, where it was first served. Over the years, the recipe has been adapted and modified, but the basic concept remains the same: thinly sliced potatoes baked until crispy on the outside and soft on the inside. The thin, accordion-like slices create a beautiful texture and make for a stunning side dish. The combination of garlic, rosemary, and Parmesan cheese adds amazing flavor to the tender and crispy potatoes.

Serves 4-6

6 large potatoes, washed and dried
4 cloves garlic, minced
3 tablespoons olive oil
3 tablespoons fresh rosemary, minced

1/2 teaspoon kosher salt
1/2 teaspoon ground black pepper
1/2 cup Parmesan cheese, grated
1/4 cup chives, chopped

Preheat oven to 400 degrees F.

Place a potato on a cutting board and cut a thin slice from the bottom of each potato to create a flat base. This will prevent the potatoes from rolling while being cut. Place a wooden spoon handle next to the potato, and use a sharp knife to make thin slits, about 1/8-inch apart, along the length of the potato, stopping about 1/4 inch from the bottom, so the slices remain connected at the bottom. Repeat with remaining potatoes.

In a small bowl, mix together the minced garlic, olive oil, and chopped rosemary. Brush the potatoes with the garlic and rosemary mixture, making sure it gets into the slits. Sprinkle salt and black pepper over the potatoes. Place the potatoes on a sheet pan lined with parchment paper and bake in the preheated oven for about 50 to 60 minutes, or until they are golden brown and crispy on the outside and tender on the inside. In the last 10 minutes of baking, sprinkle the grated Parmesan cheese on top of the potatoes.

Once the cheese has melted, sprinkle the chopped chives over the potatoes.

Note:

- Leftover Hasselback potatoes can be stored in an airtight container in the refrigerator for up to 3 days. To reheat, place them in a preheated oven at 350 degrees F for 10 to 15 minutes, or until heated through.

- Serve alongside grilled steak, chicken, or fish for a hearty meal.

- For a delicious variation, consider topping the Hasselback potatoes with crispy bacon bits or crumbled feta cheese before serving.

French Green Beans with Shallot Vinaigrette

This dish never disappoints. It combines vibrant green beans that are blanched, offering a crisp yet yielding texture. The star of the show, however, lies in the roasted shallot vinaigrette that gently envelops the beans, infusing them with an irresistible depth of oniony flavor. I usually make this during special occasions like Thanksgiving, Hanukkah, or Christmas.

Serves 4

1 pound French green beans, ends trimmed
2 large shallots, peeled and sliced
2 tablespoons extra virgin olive oil
1/4 cup extra virgin olive oil
2 tablespoons red wine vinegar
1 tablespoon Dijon mustard
1/4 teaspoon kosher salt
1/4 teaspoon ground black pepper

Preheat oven to 400 degrees F.

Place the sliced shallots on a sheet pan lined with parchment paper, drizzle with 2 tablespoons of extra virgin olive oil, and toss to coat. Roast in the oven for about 15 to 20 minutes or until the shallots are golden and caramelized. Remove from the oven and let them cool.

Bring a large pot of salted water to a boil. Add the French green beans and blanch for about 2 to 3 minutes, or until they are tender yet still crisp. Drain the beans and immediately transfer them to a bowl of ice water to stop the cooking process. Drain the beans and pat dry with a clean kitchen towel or paper towels.

In a small bowl, combine the roasted shallots, 1/4 cup of extra virgin olive oil, red wine vinegar, Dijon mustard, salt, and pepper. Whisk together until well combined and the vinaigrette is emulsified. Place the blanched green beans in a serving dish. Drizzle the roasted shallot vinaigrette over the beans and toss gently to coat them evenly. Taste and adjust the seasoning if needed.

Note:

- Blanching the green beans briefly in boiling water before transferring them to ice water helps to set their vibrant green color and preserve their texture.

- The quick cooking and cooling process helps to denature enzymes that could otherwise cause the beans to become dull and lose their crispness.

- When whisking the vinaigrette ingredients together, the Dijon mustard acts as an emulsifier, helping to bind the oil and vinegar together and create a smooth, well-incorporated dressing.

Sautéed Red Cabbage with Bacon and Gorgonzola

I love the rich, deep ruby color of this sautéed red cabbage dish, which makes it the perfect accompaniment to almost any meal. Whether I'm pairing it with a piece of sautéed chicken or a juicy grilled steak, this dish always adds a burst of color and flavor to my plate. Sauté the cabbage instead of braising it. One of the things I love most about this recipe is its versatility. You can switch out the type of vinegar I use to create different flavor profiles, whether it's tangy apple cider vinegar or nutty sherry vinegar. You can also experiment with different types of cheese to give the dish a unique twist. Sometimes, I'll use tangy feta cheese, and other times I'll opt for creamy goat cheese or nutty Parmesan.

Serves 4-6

8 slices thick-cut bacon, chopped
1 large yellow onion, chopped
1 6-inch diameter red cabbage, shredded
3 garlic cloves, minced
1/4 teaspoon kosher salt

3 tablespoons water
1/3 cup balsamic vinegar
1 tablespoon white sugar
1 teaspoon Worcestershire sauce
4 ounces Gorgonzola cheese
1 lemon

In a large pan over medium heat, cook the chopped bacon until crispy, about 5 minutes. Remove the bacon with a slotted spoon and set it aside on paper towels to drain. To the same pan, add the chopped onion and cook for about 8 minutes until softened. Add the shredded red cabbage, minced garlic, kosher salt, and water to the pan. Stir well to combine. Cook the cabbage mixture for 10 to 12 minutes until the onions and cabbage are soft. If the cabbage is not yet soft, add 2 tablespoons of water and continue cooking until it has wilted. Add the balsamic vinegar, white sugar, and Worcestershire sauce to the pan. Cook for 4 minutes, stirring well to combine.

Transfer to a serving dish and sprinkle the reserved bacon over the top of the cabbage. Place dollops of Gorgonzola on top, then squeeze half a lemon over the dish.

Note:

- Use a large pan. You'll need a large pan to sauté the cabbage, as it will take up a lot of space when raw. A 12-inch pan or larger should work well.

- The texture of cabbage can change depending on the cooking time. Sautéing the cabbage for the recommended 10 to 12 minutes ensures that it becomes soft and tender while still retaining some texture. Overcooking may result in a mushy texture, so it's important to monitor the cabbage closely during cooking.

- Gorgonzola cheese is a bold and flavorful cheese that pairs well with the sautéed red cabbage and bacon. Its creamy and slightly pungent taste complements the dish. If you prefer a milder or different cheese flavor, you can experiment with alternatives, such as blue cheese, feta, or grated Parmesan.

Roasted Cauliflower with Tomatoes and Parmesan

As a chef, I love creating recipes that are both easy to prepare and packed with flavor. This roasted cauliflower with tomatoes and parmesan is a perfect example of that philosophy. The sweetness of the cherry tomatoes and the nuttiness of the Parmesan cheese perfectly complement the mild flavor of the cauliflower, creating a delicious side dish. The recipe is simple and straightforward, requiring only a few key ingredients and minimal prep time.

Serves 4

1 head cauliflower, cut into florets
2 cups cherry tomatoes, halved
4 cloves garlic, minced
1/4 cup olive oil
1 teaspoon kosher salt
1 teaspoon black pepper

1 teaspoon dried thyme
1 teaspoon dried oregano
1/2 cup Parmesan cheese, grated
2 tablespoons balsamic vinegar
3 tablespoons chopped chives

Preheat oven to 425 degrees F.

Roasting: On a sheet pan lined with parchment paper, toss together the cauliflower, cherry tomatoes, minced garlic, olive oil, salt, pepper, dried thyme, and dried oregano. Make sure the vegetables are evenly spread out in a single layer on the sheet pan. Overcrowding the pan can lead to uneven cooking and the vegetables won't char properly. Roast in the oven for 20 to 25 minutes, or until the cauliflower is tender and the tomatoes are slightly charred. Remove the sheet pan from the oven and sprinkle the grated Parmesan cheese over the cauliflower.

Return to the oven and bake for an additional 5 minutes, or until the cheese is melted and bubbly.

Drizzle the balsamic vinegar over the roasted cauliflower and tomatoes and toss well to combine. Garnish with chopped chives before serving.

Note:

- For added texture and flavor, consider adding nuts like slivered almonds, pine nuts, or walnuts to the dish. Simply sprinkle them on top of the roasted vegetables before adding the Parmesan cheese.

- When tossing the vegetables with the balsamic vinegar, make sure they are still warm. The warmth will help the flavors blend together better.

- For added convenience, you can toss the cauliflower, cherry tomatoes, minced garlic, olive oil, salt, pepper, dried thyme, and dried oregano on the sheet pan in advance, refrigerate, and then roast when ready. This saves time on the day of cooking and allows for easy preparation.

Braised Brussels Sprouts with Bourbon Soaked Cranberries

Brussels sprouts have had a bad reputation for years due to their strong, sulfurous odor and bitter taste when cooked improperly. In this recipe, we blanch the Brussels sprouts, then shock them in ice water to keep their beautiful green color. Then, we use a braising technique to bring out the natural sweetness of the Brussels sprouts and balance it with the salty and smoky flavors of bacon. The bourbon soaked cranberries and balsamic vinegar add a rich depth of flavor, and touch of sweetness and chewiness. By braising the Brussels sprouts in chicken stock, we ensure that they cook evenly and become tender without becoming mushy.

Serves 4-6

1/2 cup dried cranberries
4 ounces bourbon
4 ounces hot water
1 1/2 pounds Brussels sprouts, cut in half lengthwise
10 slices thick-cut bacon, cut into matchsticks
1 tablespoon olive oil
1 red onion, cut in half, sliced into 1/4-inch slices

4 garlic cloves, chopped
1/2 teaspoon kosher salt
1 (15-ounce) can chicken stock
2 tablespoons of Worcestershire sauce or soy sauce
3 tablespoon balsamic vinegar
1 (6-ounce) container crispy onions, like French's

Cranberries: In a small bowl, combine the dried cranberries with the bourbon and hot water. Set aside and let the cranberries rehydrate while you prepare the rest of the dish.

Blanching Brussels: Bring a pot of salted water to a boil. Add the prepared Brussels sprouts and cook for 3 to 4 minutes until slightly tender but still crisp. Drain the sprouts and transfer them to a bowl of ice water to stop the cooking process. Once cooled, set them aside.

Cooking Brussels: In a large Dutch oven or heavy-bottomed pot, cook the bacon over medium fire until crisp. Remove the bacon with a slotted spoon and set aside, leaving the bacon fat in the pot. Add the olive oil to the pot with the bacon fat and heat over medium-high fire. Add the sliced red onion, garlic, and kosher salt and cook until softened and lightly browned, about 3 to 4 minutes. Add the Brussels sprouts to the pot and stir to coat with the onion mixture. Cook for 6 to 8 minutes, stirring occasionally, until the Brussels sprouts are lightly browned. Add the chicken stock and Worcestershire or soy sauce and bring to a simmer. Cover the pot and cook for 10 minutes until the Brussels sprouts are tender. Remove the lid from the pot and increase the heat to high. Cook for 5 more minutes, stirring occasionally, until the liquid has reduced and thickened slightly.

Transfer the cooked Brussels sprouts to a serving platter. Add the cranberries with their juices to the Brussels sprouts along with the reserved bacon and crispy onions. Drizzle the dish with balsamic vinegar for added tanginess, and sprinkle a generous handful of crispy onions over the Brussels sprouts.

Note:

- Brussels sprouts contain enzymes that can cause discoloration and off flavors when they are exposed to heat or air. Blanching helps inactivate these enzymes, preventing the sprouts from turning brown or developing unpleasant flavors during subsequent cooking methods.

- When adding the chicken stock to the pot, make sure to scrape the bottom of the pan to release any browned bits that may have formed during cooking. This will add flavor to the dish.

- If you prefer not to use bourbon, you can soak the dried cranberries in hot water or chicken stock instead.

Creamed Corn

Creamed corn, thanks to its rich, creamy texture and sweet corn flavor, perfectly complements any meal. While making creamed corn from scratch may seem daunting, it's actually a simple and easy process that requires just a few key ingredients. This recipe utilizes fresh corn, but frozen corn can be used in the same quantity, making it a versatile dish that can be enjoyed year-round.

Serves 2-4

3 tablespoons butter
1 small onion, finely chopped (1 cup)
1 jalapeno, minced, seeds and ribs removed (optional)
2 garlic cloves, minced
1 red bell pepper, minced, seeds and ribs removed
4 cups fresh corn (from about 5 ears of corn)
1/2 cup heavy cream
1/4 teaspoon crushed red pepper flakes
1/2 teaspoon kosher salt
1 tablespoon granulated sugar
3 tablespoons chopped fresh basil or tarragon
1/4 cup grated Parmesan cheese

In a pan over medium fire, melt the butter. Add the onion, jalapeño (if using). Sauté until soft and fragrant, about 3 to 4 minutes, then add the garlic and cook for 1 minute.

Add the corn kernels and the minced red bell pepper and cook for 5 to 7 minutes, stirring occasionally, until they are tender and slightly browned.

Pour in the heavy cream, red pepper flakes, kosher salt, and sugar. Bring the mixture to a simmer and let it cook for 6 minutes until the cream has thickened and coats the back of a spoon.

Stir in the chopped basil or tarragon and grated Parmesan cheese. Stir and serve immediately.

Note:

- In the recipe, we cook the cream mixture until it reaches a consistency where it coats the back of a spoon. This culinary technique is known as nappe. Nappe refers to the desired thickness of a sauce or mixture when it is thick enough to create a clear and distinct line on the spoon when a finger is run across it.

- For a slightly smoky flavor, you can grill or char the corn cobs before cutting off the kernels.

- To make this dish ahead of time, you can prepare the creamed corn mixture up to the point where you add the herbs. Let it cool to room temperature, then store it in an airtight container in the refrigerator for up to 2 days. Reheat the mixture over medium-low heat, stirring occasionally, until heated through. Stir in the chopped herbs and serve.

Garlicky Mashed Potatoes

For the most flavorful garlicky mashed potatoes, slow-cook the garlic cloves until they reach a delightful sweetness, then incorporate them into the creamy potatoes. As the aromatic garlic simmers in fragrant olive oil, its natural sugars caramelize, creating a rich and nutty flavor that elevates our mashed potatoes to new heights. This cooking technique, known as confit, ensures a heavenly taste experience that will leave your taste buds dancing with delight.

Serves 4-6

1/2 cup heavy cream
2 pounds Yukon Gold potatoes, peeled and quartered
1 tablespoon kosher salt (for the water)
1 cup garlic cloves, peeled
1 cup olive oil
1/4 cup butter
Optional:
1/2 cup grated Parmesan cheese
1 tablespoon of chopped fresh herbs
a pinch of nutmeg

Put the cream in a pan and gently warm it up, then set to the side.

Garlic confit: In a small saucepan, combine the garlic and the olive oil. Over very low fire, cook the garlic until it is tender, sweet, and fragrant, about 25 to 30 minutes. Drain the garlic and reserve the oil. Set the garlic cloves to the side.

Potatoes: Bring a large pot of water with 1 tablespoon of kosher salt to a boil. Add the potatoes to the pot and cook until you can pierce the potatoes with a fork, about 15 to 20 minutes.

Drain the potatoes well and return them to the pot on a low fire for a few minutes, stirring them gently over low heat until the excess moisture has evaporated. Remove the pot from the heat.

Pass the potatoes through a potato ricer or food mill and transfer them to a bowl. Add the warm cream into the potatoes and mix well. Mash the cooked garlic cloves and add them to the potatoes along with the butter, then mix thoroughly. Add 2 to 3 tablespoons of the reserved garlic oil to the mashed potatoes and stir it in well.

Season with salt and pepper to taste. For added flavor, stir in Parmesan cheese, herbs, or nutmeg, if desired. Serve immediately.

Note:

- To avoid a glue-like texture, it's important to warm the cream before adding it to the hot mashed potatoes.

- Use the leftover garlic-infused olive oil for cooking that week as you would any cooking oil or as a flavorful addition to dressings and marinades.

Creamed Pearl Onions with Lemon and Peanuts

When it comes to making a delicious side dish, my husband Marty always turns to his favorite recipe: creamed pearl onions with lemon and peanuts. This versatile dish not only shines as a delightful accompaniment, but Marty also loves to serve it over crispy toast points for a mouthwatering appetizer. With its modern twist, these tiny onions bring a subtle sweetness and creamy texture that beautifully complements roasted meats and grilled fish. The addition of crunchy peanuts adds a delightful texture, while a squeeze of lemon juice adds freshness.

Serves 4-6

1 (12 to 14-ounce) bag frozen pearl onions
10 ounces chicken stock
8 ounces heavy cream
2 teaspoons dried thyme
1 tablespoon lemon juice
1 teaspoon kosher salt

3-4 dashes hot sauce
1/2 teaspoon black pepper
2 tablespoons freshly chopped parsley
3 tablespoon dry roasted peanuts, chopped

Put the frozen pearl onions in a sauté pan over medium fire and cover them with the chicken stock. Cook for 8 to 10 minutes or until the onions are tender and the liquid has reduced by half.

Add the cream, thyme, lemon juice, salt, hot sauce, and black pepper.

Simmer for 10 to 15 minutes, or until the cream has thickened and coats the back of a spoon.

Remove the pan from the fire and stir in the freshly chopped parsley and chopped dry roasted peanuts.

Roasted Root Vegetables

Experience the sheer delight of Roasted Root Vegetables, a beloved household favorite from my time in Chicago. This cherished recipe became a comforting fall-back option that I turned to time and time again, always yielding exceptional results. It encapsulates the essence of simplicity and flavor, as humble ingredients are artfully transformed into a symphony of roasted goodness. The best thing about this side dish is that while it cooks, I have the opportunity to accomplish other tasks, knowing that a mouthwatering dish is taking shape.

Serves 4-6

1 large red onion, cut into 1/2-inch slices
1 1/2 pound carrots, peeled, cut into 1-inch pieces
2 pounds sweet potatoes, peeled, cut into 1-inch pieces
1 1/2 pounds baby potatoes, halved
4 garlic cloves, minced

2 tablespoons fresh rosemary, chopped
2 tablespoons fresh thyme leaves, chopped
1/2 cup olive oil
1 teaspoon kosher salt
1 teaspoon black pepper
2-3 tablespoons balsamic vinegar

Preheat oven to 400 degrees F.

Line a sheet pan with parchment paper. Place the red onion, carrots, sweet potatoes, baby potatoes, garlic, rosemary, thyme, olive oil, salt, and black pepper on the sheet pan.

Toss the vegetables until they are evenly coated with the oil and seasonings.

Spread the vegetables out in a single layer, ensuring they are not crowded.

Roast the vegetables in the oven for 30 to 40 minutes, or until they become tender and golden brown. Halfway through cooking, give the vegetables a toss to ensure even roasting. Once cooked, remove the sheet pan from the oven and drizzle the balsamic vinegar over the vegetables. Toss everything together to combine the flavors.

Note:

- To save time, you can prep the vegetables one day ahead by placing them in resealable plastic bags (excluding the olive oil, salt, pepper, and balsamic vinegar). When ready to cook, simply toss everything onto a parchment-lined sheet pan and follow the recipe.

- Spreading the vegetables out in a single layer on the sheet pan ensures that they roast evenly. If they are crowded, they may steam instead of roast, resulting in less caramelization and browning.

- Cutting the vegetables into uniform sizes ensures that they cook evenly. Different-sized pieces may require different cooking times, leading to some vegetables being overcooked or undercooked.

Cinnamon Roasted Beets with Pistachio Butter

Roasted beets have a unique combination of earthy and sweet flavors that become even more pronounced during the cooking process. To enhance their taste, I incorporate the warm and spicy notes of cinnamon. While optional, I recommend serving these beets with a delightful pistachio butter that adds nutty and fruity undertones. The combination of flavors creates a harmonious balance, with the beets complementing the nuttiness of the pistachios and the pistachios offering a contrasting texture to the beets. However, even without the pistachio butter, these beets are delicious when paired with a tangy vinaigrette.

Serves 4-6

Roasted Beets:
3 pounds beets, peeled and quartered
4 tablespoons olive oil
1 teaspoon ground cinnamon
1 tablespoon kosher salt
1 orange, zested and juiced (set the zest to the side for the vinaigrette)

Vinaigrette:
1/4 cup white wine vinegar
1/4 cup flat leaf parsley, chopped
1/4 teaspoon kosher salt
1/4 cup extra virgin olive oil

Pistachio Butter (recipe follows)

Preheat oven to 375 degrees F.

Beets: Put the peeled and quartered beets in an oven-safe baking dish. In a bowl, whisk together the olive oil, ground cinnamon, kosher salt, and orange juice. Pour the mixture over the beets and toss well to coat. Cover tightly with foil and roast in the preheated oven for 45 minutes, or until the beets are tender. While the beets are cooking, prepare the vinaigrette and pistachio butter.

Vinaigrette: In a small bowl, whisk together the white wine vinegar, reserved orange zest, chopped flat leaf parsley, and kosher salt. Slowly drizzle in the olive oil, whisking constantly, until the vinaigrette is emulsified. Set aside until the beets are done.

Pistachio Butter

1/2 cup shelled pistachios
2 tablespoons honey
2 tablespoon olive oil

1 tablespoon water
chopped romaine (optional)

To prepare the pistachio butter, start by pulsing the shelled pistachios in a food processor until they are coarsely ground. Then, add the honey and olive oil, pulsing until the mixture begins to come together. Gradually add water, one tablespoon at a time, and continue pulsing until the mixture reaches a creamy and pourable consistency.

Once the beets are roasted, carefully pour the remaining liquid from the baking dish into the vinaigrette. Whisk the liquid into the vinaigrette until well combined.

Add the roasted beets to the vinaigrette and toss them thoroughly to ensure they are well coated. Allow the beets to cool for a few minutes and then allow them to marinate in the refrigerator for at least a couple of hours, or ideally overnight. This will allow the flavors to penetrate the beets more thoroughly, resulting in a more flavorful and well-marinated final dish.

To serve, drizzle the beets with a generous amount of the pistachio butter. For an extra touch of freshness and texture, you can also add chopped romaine lettuce to the dish. While the addition of romaine is optional, it adds a delightful element that beautifully complements the beets.

Note:

- If you prefer to skip the step of roasting fresh beets, you can opt for pre-cooked beets available at the grocery store. Slice the pre-cooked beets into quarters and add them directly to the vinaigrette. Toss well to coat the beets, allow them to marinate in the flavorful dressing, and proceed with the recipe.

- If you're new to peeling beets with a vegetable peeler, it's a simple process of applying gentle pressure and sliding the peeler along the surface of the beet to remove the outer skin.

- Test the doneness of the beets by inserting a fork or skewer into the thickest part of a beet piece. If it goes in easily with little resistance, the beets are cooked. Avoid overcooking, as it can result in a mushy texture and loss of flavor.

Entrees

Entrees, the heart and soul of any meal, are a moment of culinary creativity that holds the power to create truly unforgettable dining experiences shared with loved ones and spark conversations around the table. Contrary to popular belief, entrees come in a wide range, from comforting and simple to elegantly impressive, catering to diverse tastes and occasions. In this section, I invite you to embrace the spirit of versatility and convenience, as some of the recipes feature the creative use of packaged ingredients. A prime example is the brown butter ravioli, where the richness and nuttiness of brown butter elevate the flavors of store-bought ravioli to new heights.

Let's remember that the beauty of cooking lies in the fact that you don't always need to reinvent the wheel in the kitchen. Classics, like perfectly fried chicken, remain just as delicious and relevant today as they were twenty years ago. That's the magic of timeless dishes: no matter how many trends come and go, their appeal stands strong. Within these pages, you'll discover a diverse range of cooking techniques. Hopefully, this section will serve as both inspiration and permission to use shortcuts when they suit your needs, without sacrificing the incredible taste and quality you desire. These recipes serve as both inspiration and permission to embrace shortcuts, without sacrificing the incredible taste and quality you desire.

Let these recipes ignite your imagination and spark joy as you create memorable entrees and conversations that will nourish both body and soul. It's time to savor the pleasure of good food, conversations, and the stories and traditions that come alive around the dining table.

Brown Butter Ravioli

This Brown Butter Ravioli recipe is a perfect example of how simple ingredients can come together to create a truly delicious and satisfying meal. Using store-bought ravioli and a quick brown butter sauce, this recipe is ideal for busy weeknights or a fancy dinner party. The nutty and rich flavor of the brown butter sauce pairs perfectly with the tender ravioli, and the garnish of chopped chives, toasted walnuts, and grated Parmesan adds the perfect finishing touch.

Serves 4

Brown Butter:
1/2 pound butter (2 sticks)
1 garlic clove, minced
1/4 teaspoon kosher salt
1/4 teaspoon ground black pepper
1 tablespoon soy sauce
3 1/2 tablespoons balsamic vinegar

Pasta:
1 (25-ounce) container of store bought ravioli (28 pieces)

Garnish:
3 tablespoons chives, chopped
1/4 cup toasted walnuts, chopped
1/4 cup grated Parmesan cheese

Bring a large pot of water with some salt to a boil and leave it on the stove while you make the brown butter. This way, the water will be ready for you when you cook the ravioli.

Brown Butter: Cut the butter into small pieces and place them in a medium-sized saucepan over medium heat. Cook the butter for 4 to 6 minutes, stirring occasionally, until it starts to sputter and foam. As the butter continues to cook, you'll notice the formation of tiny brown specks on the bottom of the pan, resembling black pepper, which indicate that you have successfully made brown butter. Once the foaming subsides and the butter turns a rich golden brown color, remove the pan from the heat. Add minced garlic, kosher salt, ground black pepper, soy sauce, and balsamic vinegar to the brown butter, and whisk the ingredients together until well combined. Set the brown butter aside until you are ready to use it in your recipe.

Pasta: Add the ravioli to the boiling water and cook according to the package instructions. Once the ravioli are cooked, drain them and add them to the pan with the brown butter sauce. Gently toss or stir the ravioli to ensure they are well coated with the sauce. Sprinkle the chopped chives, toasted walnuts, and grated Parmesan over the ravioli. Serve immediately.

Note:

- To truly capture the unique flavor of brown butter, make sure you don't miss those little black specks at the bottom of the pan. Those specks are what give brown butter its distinct and delicious taste, going beyond just the butterfat.

- Toss in some wilted spinach, kale, or arugula to the cooked ravioli along with the brown butter sauce. The greens will add freshness, color, and a nutritious element to the dish.

- Squeeze some fresh lemon or orange juice into the brown butter sauce after it's removed from the heat. The citrus notes will add a refreshing and vibrant element to the dish.

Beef Filet with Goat Cheese and Shallot Vinaigrette

I still remember my first experience with a filet steak vividly. It was a revelation to me, especially considering its substantial thickness compared to the minute steaks I was accustomed to. The moment I took that first bite, I was completely captivated by the explosion of flavors and the tender texture. From that moment on, I was hooked. I yearned to recreate this culinary delight at home, but there was one hurdle: I found filet steaks to be quite expensive and feared I might mess up the cooking process. If you're a steak lover and find yourself concerned about achieving the perfect level of doneness for your steak—whether it's avoiding overcooking or undercooking—I highly recommended you invest in an ovenproof meat thermometer. By using a reliable thermometer, you can effortlessly cook your steak to your desired level of doneness.

Serves 4

Roasted Shallot Vinaigrette:
3 shallots, sliced 1/4 inch thick
1 garlic clove
1 star anise (optional)
3/4 cup olive oil
3 tablespoons balsamic vinegar
2 teaspoons Dijon mustard
1/2 teaspoon kosher salt
1/2 teaspoon ground black pepper

Filet:
4 (6-ounce) beef filets
1 tablespoon kosher salt
olive oil
5 ounces baby spring mix
4 ounces goat cheese
Oven proof thermometer (If you don't have one, refer to the cooking times below for desired levels of doneness.)

Preheat oven to 325 degrees F.

Roasted Shallot Vinaigrette: Place the sliced shallots, garlic, and star anise (if using) in a large ramekin on a sheet pan and roast, uncovered, for 20 to 30 minutes until caramelized. Remove and discard the star anise. Allow the mixture to cool completely. Transfer the mixture to a small food processor, and add the olive oil, balsamic vinegar, Dijon mustard, salt, and black pepper and pulse until emulsified.

Preheat your oven to 400 degrees F to cook the filets.

Cook Filets: Rub the filets with olive oil really well and sprinkle about 1/2 teaspoon of kosher salt on both sides of each steak. Heat an ovenproof sauté pan over high heat, and sear each side of the steak for 3 minutes each. Transfer the pan with the steaks to the preheated oven. Use a meat thermometer to monitor the internal temperature of the steaks. If you don't have an ovenproof meat thermometer, you can rely on the cooking times listed below as an alternative method to achieve the desired doneness.

Medium Rare (125 degrees F) or 8 to 10 minutes
Medium (135 degrees F) or 10 to 12 minutes
Medium-Well or (145 degrees F) 12 to 14 minutes
Well-Done (160 degrees F) or 14 to 16 minutes

Once they have reached your desired doneness, let the steaks rest, covered in foil, for 8 to 10 minutes.

To Serve: Place a handful of baby greens in the center of each plate, and place a filet on top of the greens. Pour 1 to 2 tablespoons of the vinaigrette over each steak, and sprinkle with crumbled goat cheese to taste.

Note:

- Resting the meat is a critical step in achieving a tender and juicy steak. During cooking, the meat's juices are pushed towards the center. If the steak is cut immediately after cooking, these precious juices will escape onto the plate, leaving the steak dry and tough. By allowing the steak to rest for a few minutes, the juices have a chance to reabsorb into the meat, resulting in a more flavorful and tender eating experience.

- The cooking times provided in this recipe are designed for 6-ounce filets. However, please keep in mind that the thickness or weight of your steaks may vary, which can affect the cooking time. Purchasing a thermometer is the best way to make sure you cook your steak perfectly each time.

Marty's Balsamic Marinated Flank Steak

My husband Marty, who was my boyfriend at the time, used to prepare this marinated flank steak for our date nights back when we lived in Chicago. He would marinate the flank steak for several hours, allowing the flavors to develop and intensify. Once evening arrived, he would cook it on the grill and serve it accompanied by a generous serving of Garlicky Mashed Potatoes (page 94) and complemented by gin martinis. Even after all these years, Marty remains dedicated to preparing this dish for us.

Serves 4

Flank Steak:
1 (1 1/2-pound) flank steak
Marinade:
1/2 cup olive oil
1/4 cup balsamic vinegar
2 tablespoons Worcestershire sauce
2 tablespoons Dijon mustard
3 garlic cloves, minced
2 tablespoons sriracha hot sauce
1 tablespoon brown sugar
4 ounces soy sauce
Garnish:
4 scallions, minced, both green and white parts

In a bowl, combine all the marinade ingredients and mix until well combined. Place the flank steak in a resealable plastic bag along with the marinade, ensuring the steak is fully coated. Seal the bag and gently massage it to distribute the marinade evenly. Refrigerate for a minimum of 2 hours or up to 12 hours to allow the flavors to develop. When ready to grill, remove the steak from the marinade and discard the marinade. Let the flank steak sit on a plate for approximately 30 minutes to reach room temperature.

Preheat a grill to high-fire. Grill the flank steak for about 4 minutes per side for medium-rare doneness and 5 minutes per side for medium doneness.

Once the steak is cooked, remove it from the grill and let it rest on a cutting board covered with foil for 10 minutes before slicing.

Sprinkle the minced scallions over the top of the sliced flank steak and serve.

Note:

- Marinating the flank steak for several hours helps tenderize the meat and infuse it with flavor. The acids in the marinade, such as vinegar and soy sauce, help break down the proteins, resulting in a more tender steak.

- Ensure that the flank steak is fully coated in the marinade and allow it to marinate for at least 2 hours, or preferably up to 12 hours, in the refrigerator.

Roasted Chicken with Rosemary and Vegetables

Roasting a whole chicken is one of the fundamental skills every home cook should master. There's nothing quite like the aroma of a perfectly roasted chicken filling the kitchen, evoking memories of cozy family dinners and gatherings with friends. For me, the process of preparing and roasting a chicken is not only practical, but also deeply satisfying. It's a meal that can feed a crowd, be dressed up or down, and is perfect for any occasion, from a casual weeknight dinner to a special holiday feast.

Serves 4-6

- 1 (5-6 pound) whole chicken
- 4 tablespoons butter, room temperature
- 3 tablespoons fresh rosemary, minced
- 2 yellow onions, sliced 1/4 inch thick
- 6 carrots, peeled and sliced 1/2 inch thick
- 10 baby red potatoes, halved
- 4 tablespoons olive oil
- 1/4 cup white wine (optional)
- 7 teaspoons kosher salt
- 1 bunch fresh thyme
- 1 orange, cut in half
- 1 lemon, cut in half
- 5 garlic cloves

Preheat oven to 425 degrees F.

In a small bowl, mash together the butter and minced rosemary. Set it aside.

Toss the sliced onions, carrots, and halved potatoes in a roasting pan with 2 tablespoons of olive oil, white wine (if using), and 3 teaspoons of kosher salt. Remove the giblets from the chicken cavity, rinse the chicken inside and out, and pat it dry with a paper towel.

Carefully lift the chicken's breast skin and rub the rosemary butter mixture underneath. Rub the remaining 2 tablespoons of olive oil all over the chicken's exterior, then season it inside and out with the remaining 4 teaspoons of kosher salt. Place half of the thyme bunch, half an orange, half a lemon, and the garlic cloves inside the chicken cavity. Add the remaining thyme, orange, lemon, and garlic to the roasting pan with the vegetables.

Tuck the chicken legs under the body or tie them together with kitchen twine, then place the chicken on top of the vegetables in the roasting pan. Roast the chicken for 1 hour to 1 hour and 15 minutes, or until a meat thermometer inserted into the thickest part of the thigh reads 165 degrees F. Once cooked, carefully remove the chicken from the roasting pan and let it rest for 15 minutes before carving. Meanwhile, squeeze the juice from the lemon and orange into the roasting pan with the vegetables, and toss the vegetables in the pan juices. Carve the chicken and serve it with the roasted vegetables and pan juices.

Note:

- Allow the roasted chicken to rest for about 15 minutes before carving. This allows the juices to redistribute throughout the meat, resulting in a more flavorful and tender chicken.

- Season the chicken liberally with salt and any desired herbs or spices. Don't be afraid to season both the outside and the cavity of the chicken for enhanced flavor.

- Before seasoning the chicken, make sure to pat it dry with a clean paper towel. This helps remove excess moisture from the skin, allowing it to crisp up better during roasting.

Spaghetti and Ricotta Meatballs

Let me take you back to a nostalgic moment in my early twenties when I stepped into an Olive Garden restaurant with my closest buddies, Louie and John. Little did I know that this culinary adventure would leave an everlasting imprint on my taste buds, thanks to the flavors of spaghetti and meatballs. The combination of juicy meatballs and a delectable sauce created a culinary symphony that captivated my senses. Inspired by that experience, I began experimenting with my own variations of these mouthwatering meatballs, even featuring them on the menu at my restaurant. But here's the best part: you don't need to spend hours in the kitchen to enjoy this classic dish. You have the flexibility to prepare the meatball mixture in advance and choose whether to pair it with your favorite jarred tomato sauce or go the extra mile and make the sauce from scratch. The beauty of this recipe lies in its simplicity and the ability to create a memorable dinner with a little help from the store. It has become a beloved favorite among my friends, especially on cozy fall or winter weekends.

Chef Alexis Hernández

Serves 4-6

Meatballs:
8 ounces ground pork
8 ounces ground beef
1 cup ricotta cheese
4 cloves garlic, minced
1/2 cup bread crumbs
1/2 cup grated Parmesan cheese
1/4 cup fresh parsley, chopped
2 large eggs
1 teaspoon kosher salt
1/2 teaspoon ground black pepper
3/4 teaspoon dried oregano
1/2 teaspoon dried basil
1/4 teaspoon of red pepper flakes (optional)
olive oil, for cooking
kosher salt, to taste
Tomato Sauce (recipe follows)

Preheat oven 375 degrees F.

In a large mixing bowl, combine the ground pork and beef. Mix them together until well combined. Add the ricotta cheese, minced garlic, breadcrumbs, Parmesan cheese, parsley, egg, salt, black pepper, dried oregano, dried basil, and red pepper flakes (if using) to the meat mixture.

Mix everything together until evenly incorporated. You can use your hands or a wooden spoon for this step. Once the mixture is well combined, cover the bowl with plastic wrap and refrigerate for at least 30 minutes. This will help the flavors meld and make it easier to shape the meatballs. Remove the meat mixture from the refrigerator.

Take about 2 tablespoons of the mixture and roll it into a ball between your palms. Repeat this process to make about 16 meatballs, each about 2 inches in diameter. Place the meatballs on the prepared baking sheet, spacing them evenly. Drizzle a bit of olive oil over the meatballs, or lightly brush them with olive oil. This will help them brown and develop a nice crust.

Bake the meatballs in the preheated oven for 20 to 25 minutes, or until they are cooked through and nicely browned on the outside. Use your favorite store bought tomato sauce or you can make my tomato sauce from scratch (recipe follows).

Note:

- The combination of ground pork and beef in the recipe helps create a tender and flavorful meatball. The ratio of 8 ounces each of ground pork and beef provides a balance of fat content.

- Ricotta cheese adds moisture and contributes to a softer texture, while bread crumbs act as a filler and absorb excess moisture, resulting in a well-textured meatball.

- To ensure even cooking, try to make the meatballs as close to the suggested size as possible. Aim for meatballs that are approximately 2 inches in diameter.

Thick Tomato Sauce

2 tablespoons olive oil
1 medium onion, finely chopped
3 garlic cloves, minced
1 (28-ounce) can
crushed tomatoes
1 (14-ounce) can tomato sauce

1 teaspoon sugar
12 teaspoons dried basil
2 teaspoons dried oregano
1/2 teaspoon kosher salt
1/4 teaspoon red pepper
flakes (optional)

Heat the olive oil in a large saucepan or Dutch oven over medium fire. Add the chopped onion to the pan and sauté until it becomes translucent and starts to soften, about 5 minutes. Stir occasionally to prevent burning. Add the minced garlic to the pan and cook for an additional 1 to 2 minutes, stirring frequently. Pour in the crushed tomatoes, tomato sauce, and tomato paste. Stir well to combine. Add the sugar, dried basil, dried oregano, salt and red pepper flakes (if using). Stir again to incorporate all the ingredients. Reduce the heat to low and let the sauce simmer for at least 30 minutes, or up to 1 hour if you have the time. The longer it simmers, the more the flavors will develop. Serve the ricotta meatballs with the tomato sauce.

Note:

- Sautéing onions and garlic in olive oil before adding the tomatoes can enhance the flavor profile of the sauce. This step helps to develop a depth of flavor and adds aromatic qualities to the sauce.

- Aside from the basic ingredients like salt and pepper, you can add herbs and spices to enhance the flavor of your tomato sauce. Popular choices include dried basil, dried oregano, and red pepper flakes for a hint of heat.

Chicken Thighs with Hot Honey and Lemon

Chicken thighs are one of my go-to options when it comes to preparing a hearty and satisfying meal that won't break the bank. They are incredibly versatile and difficult to overcook, making them an ideal choice for cooks of all skill levels. The addition of lemon juice is particularly noteworthy, as it denatures the proteins in the chicken slightly, resulting in a tender and flavorful dish that's easy to make and perfect for family dinners. While optional, the charred lemons can add a nice pop of color and visual appeal to the dish, enhancing the overall presentation. Their caramelized edges and slightly charred appearance complement the chicken beautifully. However, feel free to omit them as the chicken thighs will still be delicious and satisfying on their own.

Serves 4-6

8 chicken thighs (bone in and skin on)
Marinade:
2 tablespoons kosher salt
1 tablespoon ground cumin
1 tablespoon ground cinnamon
1 teaspoon dried tarragon
Juice of one lemon
1/2 cup olive oil
Charred Lemon (Optional):

1 lemon sliced, into 1/4-inch wheels
1 teaspoon kosher salt
2 teaspoons extra virgin olive oil
Hot Honey Sauce:
2 lemons, juiced
2 tablespoons honey
3 teaspoons sriracha
8 garlic cloves, smashed
3 scallions, minced for garnish

Set oven to 400 degrees F.

Marinade the Chicken: To make the marinade, mix salt, cumin, cinnamon, tarragon, juice of one lemon, and 3 tablespoons of olive oil in resealable plastic bag. Squish the bag with your hand to blend the ingredients. Place the chicken in the resealable plastic bag. Close the bag and massage it to ensure that the seasonings are evenly distributed throughout the chicken and refrigerate the chicken for an hour.

Charred Lemon: Sprinkle both sides of the lemon slices with kosher salt. Heat a sauté pan over medium fire and add 2 teaspoons of olive oil. Place the lemon slices in the pan and cook for 2 to 3 minutes on each side, ensuring that the edges of the lemons are charred. Once done, remove from the pan and set aside on a plate.

Hot Honey Sauce: Pour the honey, lemon juice, and sriracha in a bowl and stir until combined. Set to the side.

Cook the Chicken: Remove the chicken thighs from the marinade bag and place them in a large sauté pan over medium fire. Add the rest of the olive oil and sauté the thighs skin side down for about 8 to 10 minutes until the skin is crispy. Then, turn the chicken over and add the smashed garlic cloves to the pan. Transfer the pan to the oven and cook for 8 to 12 minutes or until the internal temperature reaches 165 degrees F.

Place the chicken thighs on a serving platter and top with the charred lemon slices and garlic. Drizzle the drippings from the pan and some of the hot honey sauce over the chicken and serve.

Garnish with some minced scallions.

Notes:

- Marinating the chicken thighs helps to infuse them with flavor and enhance their tenderness. The acidity from the lemon juice in the marinade helps to denature the proteins in the chicken slightly, resulting in a more tender and flavorful dish.

- The charred lemon slices not only add visual appeal but also bring a slightly caramelized and smoky flavor to the dish. This step is optional but can elevate the overall taste experience.

- Searing the chicken thighs skin side down in a sauté pan before transferring them to the oven helps to achieve a crispy and flavorful skin. This dual cooking method ensures that the chicken is cooked through while still maintaining a crispy texture on the outside.

Braised Lamb Shanks

Braised lamb shanks are a classic comfort food that is perfect for cooler weather. This hearty and savory dish is a great way to enjoy tender and flavorful lamb shanks. Braising meat at 275 degrees F for a longer period of time allows the proteins to denature and unravel slowly, resulting in more tender and flavorful meat that easily falls off the bone. The collagen in the meat also slowly breaks down into gelatin, giving the meat a rich and silky texture. The result is melt-in-your-mouth lamb shank that is packed with flavor.

Serves 4

4 tablespoons olive oil
4 large lamb shanks (1 to 1 1/2 pounds total)
2 whole cloves
3 yellow onions, chopped
5 carrots, peeled and chopped
4 celery stalks, chopped
1/4 teaspoon kosher salt
4 garlic cloves, chopped

3 teaspoons dried thyme
1/4 teaspoon red pepper flakes
16 ounces white wine
2 (14.5-ounce) cans diced tomatoes, drained
2 tablespoons Worcestershire sauce
32 ounces beef broth

Preheat oven to 275 degrees F.

Heat olive oil in a large Dutch oven or oven-safe pot over medium-high fire. Season the lamb shanks generously with salt and black pepper, and then brown them on all sides in the pot. Remove the lamb shanks from the pot and set them aside. In the same pot, add cloves, chopped onions, carrots, celery, salt, garlic, dried thyme, and red pepper flakes. Cook the vegetables for 5 to 7 minutes. Pour in the white wine and cook until it's reduced by half, about 5 minutes. Add the drained diced tomatoes and Worcestershire sauce. Stir until everything is combined. Place the lamb shanks back into the pot and add the beef broth to cover only 1/2 or 3/4 of the lamb shanks. Cover the pot with a lid and transfer it to the oven. Cook for 3 1/2 to 4 hours, or until the lamb shanks are tender and falling off the bone. Remove the pot from the oven and let the lamb shanks rest for about 10 to 15 minutes before serving.

Notes:

- You can braise the lamb shanks the day before, refrigerate them in their cooking liquid, and then reheat them when you're ready to serve on the stove top on low heat. This way, you can enjoy an impressive dish without the stress of last-minute cooking.

- Braising the lamb shanks at 275 degrees F allows the collagen in the meat to break down into gelatin, resulting in tender and flavorful meat that easily falls off the bone.

Peanut Butter BBQ Ribs

At first, the thought of slathering pork ribs with peanut butter BBQ sauce may raise eyebrows, but believe me, it's an unexpectedly delightful and delicious combination. The nutty richness of the peanut butter perfectly complements the smoky tang of the BBQ sauce, resulting in a flavor explosion that even the most discerning taste buds will appreciate. During a family vacation in Key West, I prepared these ribs for my brother-in-law, Duffy, a true meat and potatoes kind of guy. He was hesitant to try them, but after one bite, he was hooked! Now, he's a frequent requester of this mouthwatering dish, proving that sometimes the most unlikely pairings can become newfound favorites.

Serves 4-6

Peanut Sauce:
3 tablespoon olive oil
2 medium onions, minced
3 clove garlic, minced
3 tablespoon freshly grated ginger
1 (14-ounce) can chopped tomatoes, drained
4 ounces soy sauce
1/4 cup dark brown sugar
1 teaspoon sriracha
1 cup creamy peanut butter
1/2 cup BBQ sauce (use your favorite brand)
4 tablespoons sesame oil

Ribs:
2 racks baby back pork ribs
6 ounces white or apple cider vinegar
kosher salt

Garnish:
3 scallions, chopped, green and white parts
3/4 cup roasted peanuts, chopped

Preheat oven to 350 degree F.

Peanut Sauce: To a large sauté pan over medium heat, add some olive oil and cook the onions until they have softened, which should take around 5 to 7 minutes. Next, add the garlic and ginger, and cook for an additional 2 minutes. Stir in the chopped tomatoes, soy sauce, brown sugar, peanut butter, BBQ sauce, and sriracha. Let the mixture simmer on low heat until the sauce has thickened, about 8 to 10 minutes. Remove the pan from the heat and let it cool slightly. Finally, add the sesame oil and give it a good stir. Set aside.

Ribs: To prepare the ribs, cut them in half and place them in a large stock pot. Fill the pot with water until it is about 4 inches above the ribs. Add 6 ounces of white vinegar and bring the water to a boil. Once boiling, reduce the heat to a simmer and cook for 45 minutes. Remove the ribs from the pot and use a fork to scrape off the membrane from the back of the ribs.

Place the ribs in a roasting pan with a V-shaped roasting rack, meat side up, and sprinkle the ribs with some kosher salt. Slather the ribs generously on both sides with the peanut BBQ sauce. Pour 1 cup of boiling water into the bottom of the roasting pan. Bake for 25 to 30 minutes, or until the BBQ sauce on the ribs is thick. You can add more sauce if you want and bake for another 20 minutes.

Remove the ribs from the oven and sprinkle chopped peanuts and scallions on top. Serve with additional sauce on the side if desired.

Note:

- Removing the membrane from the back of the ribs ensures more tender and flavorful results by allowing the BBQ sauce and seasonings to penetrate the meat, leading to ribs that easily fall off the bone during cooking.

- The simmering process with white or apple cider vinegar helps tenderize the ribs. Be patient and allow them to simmer for the full 45 minutes to achieve the desired tenderness.

- The ribs can be made 1 day ahead without adding sauce and then reheated in the oven with some water on the bottom of the pan.

- These ribs have already undergone the initial cooking process during the simmering stage, which helps make them tender and flavorful. The subsequent baking in the oven is primarily to thicken the delectable peanut BBQ sauce and allow its rich flavors to penetrate the meat. Keep in mind that the main goal in the oven is to achieve a caramelized glaze on the ribs.

Fried Chicken

For years at my restaurant, this fried chicken recipe has been a staple and a guest favorite, often served with the Garlicky Mashed Potatoes. By brining the chicken in a vinegar brine and using a double-dredging technique, you will get a juicy chicken with a crunchy crust. I've added a sweet and spicy sriracha glaze, lemon zest, and chives to the garnish. While I use boneless chicken breast exclusively, you can use any cut of chicken you prefer.

Serves 4-6

Wet Brine:
1 quart cold water
2 tablespoons white vinegar
1 tablespoon kosher salt
8 boneless chicken breasts
Sriracha Glaze:
1/2 cup honey
3 tablespoons sriracha
1 tablespoon water
1 tablespoon lemon juice
For the Dredge:
4 cups all-purpose flour
2 tablespoons dried oregano
2 tablespoons dried tarragon
2 tablespoons dried basil
2 tablespoons granulated garlic
2 tablespoons onion powder
1 tablespoon corn starch
2 tablespoons kosher salt
1 tablespoon granulated white sugar
Garnish:
zest of 2 to 3 lemons
3 tablespoons chives, minced

Brine: In a large container, combine the cold tap water, white vinegar, and kosher salt. Use a whisk to dissolve the salt and ensure the mixture is well combined. Place the boneless chicken breasts on a cutting board and cover them with plastic wrap. Gently pound the thicker side of the breast until it is the same thickness as the thinner side of the chicken breast. Cut the chicken breasts diagonally and add the chicken pieces to the brine. Cover and let it sit for at least one hour or up to 2 hours in the refrigerator.

Sriracha Glaze: Take the honey, sriracha, water, and lemon juice and mix together in a bowl; set aside.

Dredge: In a large bowl, whisk the dredge ingredients together and set aside. Dredge 3 to 4 pieces of chicken in the dredge mixture until well coated. Then, dip the chicken into the vinegar brine. Return the chicken to the dredge mixture and ensure it is fully coated.

Frying Chicken: In a large Dutch oven or deep fryer, heat vegetable oil over medium-high heat until it reaches 350 to 375 degrees F. Carefully add 3 to 4 pieces of chicken to the hot oil, making sure not to overcrowd the pan. Cook for 10 to 12 minutes, flipping halfway through. While the chicken is cooking, dredge the next batch of 3 or 4 pieces of chicken. Check the temperature of one chicken breast with a thermometer after almost 9 minutes and ensure it registers 165 degrees F. Repeat the cooking process with the remaining chicken pieces.

To serve, set the fried chicken breasts on a serving platter and drizzle sriracha glaze over each piece of chicken, then sprinkle with lemon zest and chives.

Note:

- Brining the chicken breasts in a vinegar solution helps to tenderize the meat and enhance its juiciness. The acid in the vinegar breaks down the muscle fibers, allowing the chicken to retain more moisture during cooking.

- The double-dredging method used in this recipe creates a thicker and crunchier crust on the fried chicken. The first dredge allows the wet brine to adhere to the chicken, while the second dredge ensures an even coating of the seasoned flour mixture for a crispy exterior.

- While the recipe recommends frying for 10 to 12 minutes, it's essential to use a meat thermometer to check the internal temperature of the chicken breasts. The thickest part of the chicken should reach 165 degrees F to ensure it's fully cooked and safe to eat.

- While boneless chicken breasts are recommended, you can apply the same brining and frying techniques to other cuts of chicken, such as bone-in chicken breasts or chicken thighs. Adjust the frying time accordingly based on the thickness and size of the chicken pieces.

Sautéed Peas with Bacon and Dill

As someone who cherishes quick and flavorsome recipes, I'm always on the lookout for dishes that effortlessly combine taste and simplicity. Let me introduce you to sautéed peas with bacon and dill. Hailing from Scandinavian, British, and French cuisine, this quick and easy recipe is a testament to its reputation. The smoky bacon, delicate peas, and the subtle freshness of dill, all brought together by a tangy touch of balsamic vinegar, elevate this humble dish to a sophisticated level. With its versatility and the ease of cooking everything in a single pan, it's a dish that promises both satisfaction and convenience, perfect for a cozy dinner for two or a busy weeknight feast.

Serves 2-4

8 slices thick-cut bacon, chopped
1 large yellow onion, chopped
1/2 teaspoon kosher salt
3 cloves garlic, minced
1 tablespoon Worcestershire sauce

4 tablespoons water
1 (15-ounce) bag frozen peas
1/4 teaspoon black pepper
4 tablespoons fresh dill, chopped
balsamic vinegar to drizzle

In a large sauté pan, cook the chopped bacon over medium-high fire until crisp. Remove with a slotted spoon and set aside.

Add the sliced onions to the same skillet with the bacon fat and cook over medium-high fire until soft and golden browned, about 8 to 9 minutes.

Add the minced garlic and cook for an additional minute. Stir in the Worcestershire sauce and water, scraping up any browned bits from the bottom of the pan.

Add the frozen peas, salt, and black pepper.

Cover the skillet and cook over medium fire until the peas are tender and heated through, stirring occasionally, about 5 to 7 minutes. Remove the skillet from the heat and stir in the chopped bacon and fresh dill. Drizzle with balsamic vinegar before serving.

Note:

- To preserve the vibrant green color and tender texture of peas, it's best to avoid overcooking them. Cooking them just until tender will help retain their appealing appearance and slight crunch.

- The recipe mentions cooking the onions until golden brown. This step is important as the browning process enhances the flavor of the onions by creating caramelization reactions, which add depth and complexity to the dish.

- If you don't have fresh dill on hand, you can use dried dill instead. Just use 2 teaspoons instead of 2 tablespoons.

Desserts

I am constantly captivated by the remarkable power that desserts possess—their ability to weave stories and create lasting memories that surpass even the brilliance of the most extraordinary main courses. While succulent braised lamb shanks and flavor-packed spaghetti and meatballs may rightfully claim their place at the center of attention, it is often the simplest of desserts that cast an enchanting spell, leaving an indelible impression that lingers for weeks to come.

During my culinary journey, a wise chef mentor once shared with me the secret to hosting a truly exceptional dinner party: the presence of 8 to 10 remarkable and uncomplicated desserts. That was good advice! These are the sweet sensations that have withstood the test of time, residing steadfastly in my culinary back pocket, ready to create a remarkable ending to any gathering, no matter the occasion. Hopefully these will take residence in your culinary back pocket.

Toasted Coconut Cake

Over the years, I've prepared this cake as a birthday treat for many friends, including my friend Donald, who is an absolute coconut cake aficionado. After trying this version, he declared it his all-time favorite among coconut cakes. What sets this recipe apart from traditional coconut cakes is the incorporation of toasted coconut, which lends the cake its unique character. By toasting the unsweetened shredded coconut, its natural sweetness is accentuated and its nutty flavor is enhanced, creating a delightful harmony of taste and texture. As the toasted coconut is combined with the moist cake batter, it imparts a deeper coconut flavor and adds a gentle crunchiness to every bite.

Makes 1 cake

1 cup (2 sticks) unsalted butter, room temperature
2 cups granulated sugar
4 large eggs, room temperature
1 tablespoon vanilla extract
1 teaspoon coconut extract
3 cups all-purpose flour
1 tablespoon baking powder
1/2 teaspoon kosher salt
1 1/2 cups whole milk, room temperature
1 1/2 cups unsweetened shredded coconut, toasted
Coconut Cream Cheese Frosting (recipe below)

Preheat oven to 350 degrees F.

Grease and flour two 9-inch round cake pans, and set them aside. Cut out parchment paper circles to fit the bottoms of the cake pans and place them inside of the pans.

In a large mixing bowl, cream the butter and sugar together until light and fluffy. Add the eggs, one at a time, mixing well after each addition. Stir in the vanilla and coconut extracts. In another bowl, whisk together the flour, baking powder, and salt. Gradually add the dry ingredients to the wet ingredients, alternating with the milk. Start and end with the dry ingredients. Mix until just combined.

Fold in the toasted unsweetened shredded coconut. Divide the batter evenly between the prepared cake pans. Smooth the tops with a spatula. Bake for 30 to 35 minutes, or until a toothpick inserted in the center comes out clean.

Allow the cakes to cool in the pans for 10 minutes. Once the cake layers have cooled completely, place one of the cooled cake layers on a flat surface, such as a cutting board or cake stand. Take a serrated knife and carefully slice off the domed or uneven top of the cake layer. Hold the knife parallel to the cutting surface and make a gentle sawing motion to level the top. Do the same with the other cake. Place one layer on a serving plate. Spread a generous layer of frosting on top. Place the second layer on top of the first, and spread frosting over the top and sides of the cake. Gently press the toasted unsweetened shredded coconut onto the sides and top of the cake for garnish. Refrigerate the cake for at least an hour before serving to allow the frosting to set.

Coconut Cream Cheese Frosting

Makes 4 1/2 cups

1 (8-ounce) package cream cheese, room temperature
1/2 cup (1 stick) unsalted butter, room temperature
4 cups powdered sugar, sifted
1 tablespoon vanilla extract
1 teaspoon coconut extract
pinch kosher salt
3/4 cup unsweetened shredded coconut, toasted

In a large mixing bowl, beat the cream cheese and butter together until smooth and creamy. Gradually add the sifted powdered sugar, mixing until well combined. Add the vanilla extract, coconut extract, and a pinch of salt. Beat until the frosting is smooth and fluffy.

Classic Chocolate Chip Cookie

Growing up, my exposure to cookies was limited to store-bought Chips Ahoy chocolate chip cookies. However, as I got older and went to college, I was introduced to homemade cookies through care packages sent by my friends' families. These care packages contained a variety of baked goods, including homemade chocolate chip cookies, which opened my eyes to the world of homemade cookies and the various techniques used to create different textures and flavors. My favorite remains the classic crispy edges and gooey center chocolate chip cookie. This recipe perfectly embodies that texture and flavor profile.

Makes 36-40 cookies

1 cup (2 sticks) unsalted butter, room temperature
3/4 cup granulated sugar
3/4 cup brown sugar, packed
2 teaspoons vanilla
2 large eggs, room temperature
2 1/2 cups all-purpose flour
1 teaspoon baking soda
1 teaspoon kosher salt
1/2 teaspoon baking powder
1/2 cup semisweet chocolate chips
1/2 cup milk chocolate chips
1/2 cup dark chocolate chips

Preheat oven to 375 degrees F.

Using a stand mixer, cream the butter, granulated sugar, and brown sugar together in a large bowl until light and fluffy, about 2 to 3 minutes. Add the vanilla extract, then add the eggs one at a time, beating well after each addition until fully combined. Do not add all the eggs at once.

In a separate bowl, whisk together the flour, baking soda, salt, and baking powder. Slowly add the dry ingredients to the wet ingredients, mixing until just combined. Fold in the chocolate chips. Take the dough, roll it into a disk, and wrap it in plastic. Let it rest in the refrigerator for 2 hours or overnight. Resting the dough allows the gluten to break down and relax, resulting in a more tender and chewy texture for the cookies.

When you are ready to bake, remove the dough from the refrigerator and let it sit at room temperature for a few minutes to soften slightly.

Using a #40 scoop (1 1/2 tablespoon cookie scoop), portion the dough onto a sheet pan lined with parchment paper, spacing the cookies about 2 inches apart.

Bake for 12 to 15 minutes or until the edges are lightly golden brown. Cool on the baking sheet for 5 minutes before transferring them to a wire rack to cool completely.

Note:

- Using room temperature butter is important in cookie baking. Softened butter will create a smoother and creamier dough, which allows for better incorporation of air during creaming, resulting in lighter and more tender cookies.

- Creaming the butter and sugars together until light and fluffy is essential for incorporating air into the dough. This step creates aeration, leading to a lighter texture in the final cookie.

- The cookie dough is great for making ahead and freezing. To freeze, portion the cookie dough onto a baking sheet and freeze until solid, then transfer to a resealable freezer bag. When ready to bake, simply place the frozen dough onto a lined baking sheet and bake as directed, adding an additional 2 to 3 minutes to the baking time.

Flan

In many Latin American and Hispanic households, including my own, flan is traditionally prepared with condensed milk as a key ingredient. However, in this adapted version of my mother's flan recipe, I use granulated sugar instead of condensed milk for the delicate, sweet, elegant profile it provides. This substitution brings a luscious creaminess and a distinctively sweet flavor to the flan.

Makes 6

1 cup granulated sugar
1/4 cup water
16 ounces heavy cream
8 ounces whole milk
zest of one lemon
1 pinch kosher salt

1/2 cup granulated sugar,
plus 1 tablespoon
4 large eggs
4 large egg yolks
1 teaspoon vanilla extract

Preheat oven 325 degrees F.

In a small saucepan, combine 1 cup of granulated sugar and water. Cook over medium heat, stirring occasionally, until the sugar dissolves and turns golden brown. Be careful not to burn it. Once caramelized, immediately pour the hot caramel evenly into the bottom of six 6-ounce ceramic ramekins, swirling to coat the bottom evenly. Set them aside.

In a separate saucepan, heat the heavy cream, milk, and lemon zest and a pinch of kosher salt over medium fire until the milk starts to steam. Set the pan to the side.

In a mixing bowl, whisk together 1/2 cup granulated sugar, eggs, egg yolks, and vanilla extract until well combined. Slowly pour the warm cream mixture into the egg mixture, whisking constantly, until fully incorporated.

Place the ramekins in a baking dish large enough to hold the six ramekins. Divide the custard mixture evenly among the prepared 6-ounce ramekins, pouring it over the hardened caramel. Carefully pour hot water into the baking dish, creating a water bath that reaches halfway up the sides of the ramekins. Carefully transfer the baking dish to the preheated oven and bake for approximately 45 to 50 minutes. If the edges are firm, and the center is slightly jiggly, the flan is likely done.

Remove the ramekins from the water bath and let them cool to room temperature. Once cooled, cover and refrigerate for at least 4 hours or overnight to allow the custards to fully set.

To serve them, run a knife around the edges of each ramekin and invert onto serving plates to release the flans with the caramel on top.

Note:

- When pouring the hot caramel into the ramekins, swirl them gently to coat the bottom evenly. This will create a beautiful caramel layer on top of the flan once it's inverted for serving.

- A pinch is 1/16 to 1/8 of a teaspoon. It literally is a tiny pinch.

- To add a crunch, top each serving of flan with a sprinkling of toasted nuts, such as almonds or pistachios. It adds a delightful texture contrast to the smooth custard.

Mock Apple Pie

I first learned about this recipe from my mother-in-law Mary. When she told me she was going to make a pie out of crackers, I was skeptical, to say the least. But as soon as I tasted it, I was blown away by the delicious combination of flavors and textures. The buttery, flaky crust pairs perfectly with the sweet and spicy filling made from sugar, cinnamon, nutmeg, and allspice, and the lemon zest adds a zing of citrusy freshness. The remarkable thing about this recipe is that despite the absence of apples, the pie looks and tastes just like it has apples in it.

Serves 4-6

1 cup water
1 stick butter
3/4 cup white sugar
1/4 cup dark brown sugar
2 teaspoons cream of tartar
1 teaspoon cinnamon
1/2 teaspoon nutmeg
1 teaspoon allspice

1 teaspoon cloves
zest of 1 lemon
juice of one lemon
3/4 teaspoon vanilla extract
18 saltine crackers
1 store-bought frozen deep dish pie crust

Preheat oven 425 degrees F.

In a medium saucepan, combine all ingredients except the saltine crackers and bring to a boil. Cook for about 2 minutes, or until the sugar has completely dissolved. Take the saucepan off the fire and add the vanilla extract.

Next, gently split the saltine crackers in half and arrange them in a frozen pie shell. Pour the hot sugar mixture over the crackers.

Place the pie on a sheet pan lined with parchment paper and bake in a preheated oven at 425 degrees F for 15 minutes. Then, reduce the oven temperature to 375 degrees F and bake for an additional 15 to 20 minutes, or until the pie is golden brown and set. If you notice that the crust is getting too dark, you can cover it with aluminum foil to prevent it from burning.

Allow the pie to cool completely at room temperature and then allow it to rest in the refrigerator for about 1 hour. Consider serving it with some freshly whipped cream on top.

Note:

- When the hot sugar mixture is poured over the saltine crackers in the pie shell, the cream of tartar helps to soften and dissolve the crackers slightly. As a result, the crackers take on a texture and appearance similar to cooked apples, giving the illusion of apples in the pie when there are actually no real apples used.

- Cream of tartar also breaks down the sugar in the recipe into simpler forms like glucose and fructose, the same as the sugar that is found in apples.

Olema's Caramel Flan Cake

Combining two of my favorite desserts into one, the flan and cake, is truly magical. During a trip to Key West with friends, my longtime friend Olema introduced me to a dessert called flancocho. Using a store bought cake mix and a flan recipe, Olema showed me how to create a spectacular, show-stopping dessert. The layering effect in flan and cake is due to the differences in density between the two layers. The flan layer is typically denser and has a higher moisture content compared to the cake layer. During baking, the cake layer rises and becomes less dense, while the flan layer remains dense, resulting in the layering effect when the cake is flipped over. The best part of this recipe is that it is made using a store bought cake mix.

Makes 1 cake

3 tablespoons butter, room temperature (for greasing Bundt pan)
Caramel:
1 cup sugar
2 tablespoons water
Cake:
1 box chocolate cake mix
1/4 cup ground cornmeal

Flan:
1 (12-ounce) can evaporated milk
1 (14-ounce) can sweetened condensed milk
3 ounces cream cheese, room temperature
5 large eggs, room temperature
1 tablespoon dark rum
2 teaspoons vanilla extract
2 teaspoons almond extract

Preheat oven to 350 degrees F.

Fill a pot with water, bring it to a boil, then set it to the side. This will be for the bain-marie we need to make for the flancocho.

Grease a 12-cup Bundt pan with the butter and set aside near the stove.

Caramel: In a saucepan, put the water and the sugar over medium fire and swirl the pan until the sugar becomes amber and almost dark. Immediately pour it into the Bundt pan. Swirl the pan once so that the caramel clings to the bottom and sides of the pan. Set it aside.

Cake: Make the boxed cake mix according to the manufacturer's instructions. Add the corn meal and combine. Then pour the cake mixture in the Bundt pan on top of the caramel.

Flan: Blend all the flan ingredients until smooth, then pour the mixture carefully over the cake batter in the Bundt pan. Place the Bundt pan in a large baking pan on the counter near the stove and add boiling water until the Bundt pan is covered halfway. Cover the Bundt pan with foil and bake at 350 degrees F for 1 hour and 30 minutes or until a toothpick inserted in the center comes out clean.

Let it cool completely, about 5 to 6 hours, before flipping to prevent the cake from breaking apart when flipped. Loosen the edges of the flancocho with a knife, place a large serving platter on top of the Bundt pan, and carefully flip both together. Remove the Bundt pan, allowing the caramel to drizzle down the sides. Keep the unserved portions covered in the refrigerator.

Note:

- The water bath (bain-marie) is essential for creating the perfect flan layer in this cake. It helps the flan cook evenly and prevents it from curdling or developing a rubbery texture. Make sure the water is boiling before adding it to the roasting pan to ensure a consistent temperature during baking.

- Patience is key when flipping the flancocho. Allow it to cool completely before attempting to flip it to avoid any mishaps. The cake needs time to set and hold its shape, making it easier to release it from the Bundt pan without breaking.

- You can prepare the flancocho in advance and keep it covered in the refrigerator until ready to serve. The flavors often meld together and improve with time, making it a convenient dessert for parties or gatherings.

Chocolate Brownies

During my grade school days, brownies were a common treat for celebrating birthdays, but I wasn't a fan of those versions. It was only after I moved to Chicago in 1988 that I stumbled upon a bakery offering truly exceptional brownies. With their crackly tops and moist centers, they left a lasting impression on me. Inspired by those bakery brownies, I decided to recreate them at home after culinary school, adding espresso powder to enhance the chocolate flavors without giving a strong coffee taste.

Chef Alexis Hernández

Serves 6-8

1 cup (2 sticks) butter
1 1/4 cup sugar
3/4 cup unsweetened cocoa powder
1 tablespoon instant coffee powder
1 teaspoon vanilla extract

3 large eggs
1 cup all-purpose flour
1/2 teaspoon baking powder
1/2 teaspoon kosher salt
1 cup semisweet chocolate chips
powdered sugar for dusting

Preheat oven to 350 degrees F.

Grease a 9-inch square baking pan. Melt the butter in a medium saucepan over low heat. Add the sugar, cocoa powder, and instant coffee powder and whisk until smooth. Remove from heat. Whisk in the vanilla extract and eggs, one at a time, until the mixture is smooth. Sift in the flour, baking powder, and salt and stir until just combined. Fold in the chocolate chips. Pour the batter into the prepared baking pan and smooth the top with a spatula. Bake for 25 to 30 minutes, or until a toothpick inserted in the center comes out with a few moist crumbs attached.

Allow the brownies to cool in the pan for 20 minutes before dusting with powdered sugar, slicing, and serving.

Note:

- The ratio of fat (butter) to sugar plays a significant role in determining the texture of brownies. A higher fat-to-sugar ratio results in fudgier brownies, while a lower ratio yields cakier brownies. In this recipe, the 1 cup of butter to 1 1/4 cups of sugar strikes a good balance, providing a moist and tender texture.

- Sifting the dry ingredients, such as cocoa powder, flour, and baking powder, helps break up lumps and ensures even distribution of these ingredients in the batter. This results in a smoother and more uniform texture in the finished brownies.

- Feel free to customize the brownies by adding chopped nuts, chocolate chips, or other mix-ins of your choice.

Citrus Vanilla Bundt Cake

The modified chiffon method I used here and extra egg yolks and butter create a lighter texture and richer flavor in the final product. With the addition of the bright and tangy citrus flavors and sweet vanilla aroma, this cake can be both buttery and citrusy without the typical heaviness of traditional pound cakes. The result is a delicious and satisfying cake with a complex and well-balanced taste and mouth feel.

Serves 6-8

- 2 teaspoons granulated white sugar
- 2 cups cake flour
- 2 teaspoons baking powder
- 1/2 teaspoon baking soda
- 1/2 teaspoon kosher salt
- 1 1/2 cups granulated sugar
- zest of 2 lemons
- zest of 1 large orange
- 1/2 cup vegetable oil
- 7 large eggs, room temperature and separated
- 1/2 cup orange juice
- 1/2 cup lemon juice
- 1 teaspoon vanilla extract
- confectioners' sugar for dusting

Preheat oven to 325 degrees F.

Prepare Bundt Pan: Lightly coat a 10-inch Bundt pan with nonstick cooking spray and dust it with flour, tapping out any excess. Sprinkle 2 teaspoons of granulated sugar into the greased Bundt pan and rotate it so that the sugar coats most of the surface.

Prepare Batter: In a medium bowl, whisk together the cake flour, baking powder, baking soda, and salt. Set aside. In a large mixing bowl, whisk together the granulated sugar, lemon zest, orange zest, vegetable oil, and egg yolks until pale and creamy, about 2 to 3 minutes. Add the orange juice, lemon juice, and vanilla extract, and whisk until smooth.

Gradually add the flour mixture to the egg mixture, whisking until just combined.

Beating Egg Whites: In a separate bowl, using an electric mixer, beat the egg whites on medium-high speed until stiff peaks form, about 3 to 5 minutes.

Combine Batter and Egg Whites: Gently fold the egg whites into the batter until no white streaks remain. Pour the batter into the prepared Bundt pan and smooth the top with a spatula.

Baking Cake: Bake until a toothpick inserted in the center comes out clean, about 50 to 60 minutes.

Chef Alexis Hernández

Cool the cake in the pan for 30 minutes before inverting onto a wire rack to cool completely. Dust the cake with confectioners' sugar before serving.

Note:

- To ensure even mixing and a better texture, make sure all ingredients are at room temperature before starting to bake. If your eggs are cold, place them in warm water for 5 to 10 minutes to bring them to room temperature.

- Add a glaze: A simple glaze made with powdered sugar and lemon juice can add an extra layer of flavor to the cake. Mix together 1 cup of powdered sugar and 2 to 3 tablespoons of lemon juice until smooth, then drizzle over the cooled cake.

Roasted Pears with Blue Cheese and Honey

When late summer rolls around and these beautiful Bosc pears are in season, I make this dessert because it's easy to make, the flavors are comforting, and they provide the perfect ending to a meal. The pairing of blue cheese and pears is not new, but roasting the pears with fresh thyme, then stuffing them with a mixture of blue cheese, nuts, and sugar takes this classic flavor combination to the next level.

Chef Alexis Hernández

Serves 6

Blue Cheese Mixture:
1/2 cup crumbled blue cheese
1/4 cup walnuts, chopped
2 teaspoons dark brown sugar
Pears:
3 medium-sized Bosc or Anjou pears
2 tablespoon olive oil
6 teaspoons granulated white sugar
2 teaspoon fresh thyme leaves, chopped
Topping:
1 tablespoon honey
1-2 tablespoons balsamic vinegar
1 tablespoon freshly chopped thyme leaves
Freshly ground black pepper

Preheat oven to 375 degrees F.

Blue cheese mixture: In a bowl, mix together the blue cheese, walnuts, and dark brown sugar; set aside.

Roast Pears: Cut the pears in half lengthwise, and remove the core and seeds with a small spoon or knife. Brush the cut side of the pears with olive oil, and add one teaspoon of white sugar over the top of each pear with some fresh thyme leaves. Place the pears cut side down on a sheet pan lined with parchment paper and roast for about 20 to 25 minutes, or until the pears are tender and golden brown. Remove the pears from the oven, and flip them over so that they are cut side up. Spoon the blue cheese mixture into the cored out area of each pear half. Drizzle each pear half with honey. Return the baking sheet to the oven and roast the pears for an additional 5 to 7 minutes until the cheese is melted and bubbly. After removing the pears from the oven, place them on plates and drizzle them with balsamic vinegar, sprinkle with freshly chopped thyme leaves, and add a few grinds of freshly ground black pepper.

Note:

- When cutting the pears in half and removing the core and seeds, be gentle to avoid damaging the pear's shape. A small spoon or melon baller can be useful for coring without losing too much flesh.

- Serve the warm roasted pears as a topping for vanilla ice cream or gelato. The contrast of temperatures and flavors is sure to be a hit.

- The recipe serves 4, but you can easily adjust the quantities to accommodate more or fewer servings.

Mini Upside-Down Pineapple Cakes

As a contestant on the Food Network's Cutthroat Kitchen, I faced a unique challenge from Chef Eric, who sabotaged me by forcing me to prepare these desserts on a hammock. It was a difficult task to make these Mini Upside-Down Pineapple Cakes as the hammock kept moving around, making it challenging to mix and pour the batter. Nevertheless, I persisted and successfully created these treats. Serve them with a dollop of whipped cream to enhance their flavor and presentation.

Serves 6

Caramel:
3/4 cup sugar
1/4 cup water
1 teaspoon vanilla extract
Cake:
1 (15-ounce) can pineapple slices
6 maraschino cherries
8 tablespoons butter, room temperature
1/4 cup sugar

2 eggs, room temperature
1 teaspoon vanilla
3/4 cup all-purpose flour
3 tablespoons uncooked grits (not instant)
1 teaspoon baking powder
1/4 teaspoon kosher salt
1/2 teaspoon ground cinnamon
2 teaspoons ground ginger

Preheat oven to 350 degrees F.

Grease 6 mini 3-inch cake molds with butter and place them on a parchment-lined sheet pan.

Separate the juice from the pineapple slices and set aside.

Caramel: In a saucepan, combine 3/4 cup of sugar and 1/4 cup of water over medium heat, stirring until sugar is dissolved. Increase heat to high and boil without stirring until the mixture turns dark brown, about 8 to 10 minutes. Remove from fire and stir in 1 teaspoon of vanilla extract. Pour the caramel evenly into the molds, then set aside. Place one pineapple slice in each mold and top with one maraschino cherry in the center.

Cake: Using a hand mixer, cream 8 tablespoons of butter and 1/4 cup of sugar until light and fluffy. Add 1 egg and stir until combined. Repeat with the second egg. Stir in 1 teaspoon of vanilla extract.

In a separate bowl, whisk together the rest of the ingredients. Gradually add the dry ingredients to the wet ingredients and mix until the batter is formed, about 2 minutes.

Fill the molds 3/4 full with the batter and bake for 20 to 25 minutes or until a toothpick inserted in the center comes out clean.

Let the cakes cool, then flip them over onto a serving plate. Using a brush, apply the reserved pineapple juice over the top and sides of the cakes. Enjoy these treats either on their own or with a dollop of whipped cream on top.

Note:

- When combining the wet and dry ingredients for the cake batter, avoid overmixing. Over-mixing can lead to tough cakes due to overdeveloping the gluten in the flour. Mix until just combined for a tender texture.

- If you don't have mini cake molds, you can also use muffin tins to make smaller versions.